**5D**

*Stephen Shaw*

# 5D

First published in the United Kingdom in 2014 by Stephen Shaw

Cover art by Deborah Grieves - http://cynnalia.deviantart.com

Publisher and author website and contact details:
www.i-am-stephen-shaw.com



ISBN: 978-0-9568237-9-3

# Stephen Shaw's Books

**Visit the website**: www.i-am-stephen-shaw.com

**I Am** contains spiritual and mystical teachings from enlightened masters that point the way to love, peace, bliss, freedom and spiritual awakening.

**Heart Song** takes you on a mystical adventure into creating your reality and manifesting your dreams, and reveals the secrets to attaining a fulfilled and joyful life.

**They Walk Among Us** is a love story spanning two realities. Explore the mystery of the angels. Discover the secrets of Love Whispering.

**The Other Side** explores the most fundamental question in each reality. What happens when the physical body dies? Where do you go? Expand your awareness. Journey deep into the Mystery.

**Reflections** offers mystical words for guidance, meditation and contemplation. Open the book anywhere and unwrap your daily inspiration.

**5D** is the Fifth Dimension. Discover ethereal doorways hidden in the fabric of space-time. Seek the advanced mystical teachings.

**Star Child** offers an exciting glimpse into the future on earth. The return of the gods and the advanced mystical teachings. And the ultimate battle of light versus darkness.

**The Tribe** expounds the joyful creation of new Earth. What happened after the legendary battle of Machu Picchu? What is Christ consciousness? What is Ecstatic Tantra?

**The Fractal Key** reveals the secrets of the shamans. This handbook for psychonauts discloses the techniques and practices used in psychedelic healing and transcendent journeys.

Something is wrong. Very, very wrong.

My world is falling apart. The name of my planet is Mani, which means 'jewel', and I remember it as a perfect glowing orb graced with tree-lined mountains, lush forests, sparkling rivers and gleaming oceans. A magnificent blue-green gem revolving around an enormous sun – the star called Arcturus.

The air was always pure and fresh, the soil unsullied by pollution. I know. I am one of the planetary leaders charged with maintaining the Cosmic Energy Shield.

I gaze around me and see nothing but death and destruction. Billows of dark smoke blemish our immaculate cities. People huddle in the streets. The natural peace is skewered by insistent wailing. Grief hangs in the air, a heavy musty blanket suffocating the scurrilous survivors.

We are at war with an unseen enemy. Our highly advanced technology appears to have failed. The Cosmic Energy Shield has faltered. A dark force permeates our world, stalking our hopes and dreams. People talk in whispers as if nefarious beings might overhear them. What has happened?

Truth is, most people remember a different history to me. A different time line. I have conflicting and confusing memories but refuse to succumb to the falsehood growing within me. I am not crazy. I am a planetary leader and will not forget my origins.

The northernmost point of our planet hosts both the Pagoda, an enormous multi-tiered building housing the Planetary Government, and the crystal Temple of Arcturus, home of the Galactic Government. A shimmering bridge connects the two structures.

Although our planet is named Mani, all beings in this world are called Arcturians, after our sacred star. Only the wisest and most virtuous Arcturians are considered for positions at the Temple of Arcturus. The highest level of the Galactic Government comprises ten Supreme Galactic Leaders, one secretive Time Lord, and a Light Seer linked to the Universal Council of Light.

I have only had the privilege of liaising with Galactic Leader Savitri, and this is the one I now seek. He must have the answers. I am desperate for an explanation.

Running through the storm of grey dust that taints our buildings and cloaks our streets. Standing still is risky. Harm lurks in every corner. Must reach the Temple.

Threatening figures ahead. Darting down a side street. Avoiding the chattering beggar. Recognise his distinctive long ragged robe. He sure gets around.

Air violently wrenched. Ground shaking. Shocked. Explosions in the distance. Temple ripped apart. Shards flying everywhere. No! No, no, no! This can't be happening.

Hand on my shoulder. Pulled into a doorway. *Crouch here. You'll be safe.*

Stunned for a moment. It's the beggar. Notice his bloodied leg. "You need help, my friend."

*Too late for me. Not for you.*

"What do you mean?"

*The Galactic Leaders now all deceased. My injuries severe.*

"No. That cannot be."

*Someone needs to pick up the mantle.*

"What mantle?"

*You are a leader, are you not?*

"I am."

*Are you a virtuous man? Do you understand impeccability?*

"My first allegiance is to Light, Love and Truth."

*Good answer. Do you wish to see your wife again?*

"How do you know about my wife? No one else remembers her."

*Your memories are real. History has been altered.*

"What are you talking about?"

He looks deep into my eyes. *Indra, I am the Time Lord.*

I step back, astounded.

Reaching into his robe, producing a small silver-blue key. All rather surreal. Handing it to me. Antique – ancient artefact – defunct in our world. What use now? Turning it over. Decorative grip. The word 'ekam' inscribed on the blade.

*The grip, the part that sits outside the lock, is called the bow. The part you insert is called the blade.*

Got one right at least. Is this a beggar's delusion or is it real? Respectful caution is probably the safest choice.

"What must I do with this?"

*It's a Time Key. Go back and fix the time line.*

"Time line?"

*Somebody went back and changed an event, creating a ripple in the time line. Altered our history.*

My brow furrows. "Seriously?"

*How else do you explain your memories? Arcturians are the leaders of the galaxy. Our world is serene and pristine. You are married. Yet here you are alone and the world is crumbling around you.*

It's the first answer that has made sense. I relax a little.

*You need to leap into the Time Stream and locate the altered time line.*

Way out of my depth. "What exactly is a Time Stream?"

*The coalescence of all time lines, of course.*

I nod, trying to appear like I understand.

"Wait a minute … Isn't time travel illegal?"

*Indeed. And for good reason. However, those that banned it are gone. It's just you and me.*

The beggar grabs my hand in a vice-grip. Strange rush of energy. Feel dizzy … disoriented …

*Did you really think the key was enough?*

"Uh … what just happened?"

*Look around. What do you see?*

Rubble … debris … smoke … dust … a door lit up with undulating blue waves. "What the –?"

*Consider yourself deputised.*

"Is this the door to the Time Stream?"

*One of many doors. You now have the ability to see.*

"And the key?"

*Insert into lock. Turn left. Always left.*

"Um … you coming?"

*Only the holder of the key may travel.*

"What about you?"

*My time is at an end.*

I hesitate, unsure about proceeding.

More explosions, closer this time.

*What are you waiting for, Indra? Your planet is about to be annihilated.*

I take a deep breath, insert the key and step through the door.

* * *

Gushing watery vortex. Shimmering waves of blue-white energy. Slipping along a large undulating tunnel. No sense of control. Shouting. Arms flailing uselessly.

The waves are multi-directional ... lost and flowing ... Which way am I going? ... How do I move?

Eventually I calm down and surrender. The strange beggar flits into my mind. His real name is Cronus. However, everyone refers to him as the Time Lord. Perhaps only his mother calls him by his real name. I imagine her shrill voice calling a young Cronus; for some reason it amuses me.

The terrible state of my world. Wonder what's happening. Instantly a glowing door appears, bearing the name of my planet, the date and the time. It's now! Tentatively I push open the door. No key required for exit it seems.

I am back amid the rubble. Cronus lies unmoving. Faint pulse. A glimmer in his light blue eyes. The hint of a smile.

*You are consciousness and your intention directs your journey.*

I nod kindly.

Last breath. He's gone. I want to cry but I don't really know him. Perhaps I am grieving for my world. In the distance a thundering noise. A most dreadful sound.

I insert the key. Step through the door. And don't look back.

***

No idea where to begin. I am on my own now. Consciousness. Thought. Intention.

It's like a mad chaotic dream. Strands oscillating along here, filaments pulsing over there. Embedded hints flowing in every fibre. Miniscule images flashing briefly on the periphery.

Impulsively I grab a filament (or is my consciousness doing that?) and am catapulted into starry space. Have I just exited the Time Stream? I panic for a moment. Where's the door?

Seek the blue waves. There! Insert key, turn left.

Alright. These are obviously the time lines. Will take more care.

Must focus my intention ... my wife Priya ... In my recent reality she did not exist but I know she is real. I must see her again. Is that selfish? My planet is being destroyed!

I have to know. Rushing along the tunnel until a door magically appears. Open it, peer through. There she is! There we are. Newly married, first year under our belt, walking hand-in-hand along one of our beautiful avenues. If I step through, they will see me. He will see me!

What are the rules? If my past self sees his future self surely that will create a ripple in the time line? Will it alter history? Hmm ... this is complicated. Cronus had insufficient time to teach me everything.

Perhaps I need to limit my intervention in the past to only the most strategic events.

I slip through the door and purchase a hooded robe in the marketplace. A sufficient disguise considering that Arcturians all have very similar bodies. In fact, our bodies are genetically engineered clones. Perfect strength, perfect health and optimal brain function. Is clone the right word? Arcturian bodies have no sex organs; as such we use gender terms tentatively. We make love in a spiritual energetic way, co-creating a new life form when appropriate. Our bodies last for approximately 500 years.

Ah, they are separating. Priya is meandering toward the entertainment sector. I have missed her! Those gorgeous almond-shaped eyes. I have to smile. All our eyes look the same. Our hairless bodies are 1.8 metres tall (6 feet in ancient measurement), slender, with greenish skin and beautiful large black eyes. Three fingers on each hand is not a limitation as our advanced brains are naturally telekinetic and telepathic. We communicate verbally only when necessary.

She is lingering outside the weird store. Blacked out windows. No sign. The Dark Shop, we used to call it. Still gives me the shivers. Always gave it a wide berth. What is she doing? Don't go in there!

I dart into a dusky corner and peruse the curious trinkets. The shop assistant looks at me strangely. Priya announces herself and is escorted to an adjoining room. My heart begins racing. I have no choice but to cloud the assistant's mind. She is younger and less experienced than me. It takes a few furtive seconds then I slip into the next room. Hopefully I won't get caught.

The energy immediately makes me feel uneasy. Standing behind the thick red curtain, I listen to Priya asking for her fortune to be read. Unusual hissing sound. I catch snippets of the peculiar whisper: "… meant for so much more … work in Temple … serve the Galactic Leaders … great burden and mission …"

It's enough. On the way out I ask the assistant for the clairvoyant's name. "Apep. I shouldn't tell you this but he also calls himself the Dark Lizard."

Priya visits the Dark Shop numerous times during the ensuing weeks. One day I witness an uncomfortable conversation. Priya is begging Indra to use his friendship with Galactic Leader Savitri to leverage an apprenticeship at the Temple. It is not long before Priya is working part-time as an administrator in the Galactic Government.

It all seems quite harmless. Perhaps I should leave this time-place. My planet needs saving and I can't see any connection here. I wish to experience a tender moment with Priya before I depart. Her name means 'beloved'. I heave a sigh. That describes exactly what she means to me.

I decide to wait until Indra's regular visit to one of the technology outposts. He usually travels alone and is gone for a couple of days. Pretending to be Indra from this reality, I should be able to have a few words with Priya without upsetting the time line. The opportunity finally presents itself and I catch her outside the Temple. It's risky but I figure we can spend an hour together.

Priya is chatting to a colleague and I am waiting patiently for her to finish. My intense focus blinds me to the approaching Galactic Leader Savitri. Frozen for a millisecond, I beam a welcoming smile. His demeanour is relaxed and sociable.

*Those two appear to have become close. Most unusual.*

"Who is the new friend?"

*It's the Time Lord's daughter, Maya.*

"Why is that unusual?"

*Maya is as reclusive, stubborn and quick-tempered as her secretive father. She doesn't make friends easily.*

"Aha."

*I have an appointment. Good to see you.*

"Peace be with you."

*Always.*

I am finally alone with Priya. We take a stroll down a sunlit path in the magnificent Temple Gardens. Rows of colourful flowers cascade along the majestic trees. I touch her hand. "Just wanted to say how much I love you." She smiles sweetly.

We reach our favourite bench near the Grand Fountain. A soft breeze caresses our relaxed bodies. Hazy rainbows dance across the streams of water. In this precious moment words are merely noise. After a long while I stand and enjoy a luxurious stretch. Priya shifts to a more comfortable position. Her clutch bag drops to the ground, spilling its contents. In a second I spot the key and levitate it before me.

"What's this? An ancient key?"

"Oh, it's nothing. I found it in the Temple. Antiquated rubbish."

Silver-blue, strikingly familiar. I examine the blade for an inscription. Ah, the word 'treeni'.

"Why are you keeping it?"

She shrugs. "Entertainment value. Curiosity. Aren't you supposed to be visiting an outpost?"

"Yes. I really should leave."

The long-overdue embrace fills my heart. We kiss tenderly. I feel torn. A sinking sensation engulfs my being. Arcturians don't tell untruths but Priya is concealing something.

And yet, so am I.

* * *

The keys are identical. Is it a coincidence? Did I accidentally choose this time-place? Did it choose me? How does time travel work? Is someone influencing my choices?

What is Priya planning? Is she an innocent bystander? Friends with the reclusive Time Lord's daughter and now possesses a Time Key. She must know what she is doing.

I obviously cannot leave now.

The next day Priya visits the Dark Shop. She is in there for hours. Eventually I enter. Nothing. There is nothing in the shop. No merchandise. No Arcturians. Nothing.

I stare at the emptiness. What has happened? Where did everything go? Why don't I have the shivers anymore?

Stupefied, I walk to the Temple. Only authorised personnel are allowed inside. Emboldened, I announce myself at the Gateway and demand to see Galactic Leader Savitri. Eventually he emerges, looking flustered and a bit concerned.

"My deepest apologies, Savitri. This is going to sound strange. I am from the future. Our planet is in danger. I need your help."

A momentary pause. His eyes close as he makes the connection. Indra is verified as being on the other side of the planet. For the very first time I am welcomed into the Temple.

I share my knowledge, swearing him to secrecy in order not to alter the time line. Then it hits me. This is the exact beginning of the alteration of our history. Priya has a Time Key and has disappeared with Apep. Who is Apep? I have now also interacted with Galactic Leader Savitri. All these actions are affecting the time line.

He is silent for a long while, finger touched to his thoughtful lips.

*This is why we banned time travel. Fraught with complicated and dangerous possibilities.*

I nod respectfully and wait.

An aide is beckoned. Brief conversation, instructions are given, then he is despatched.

*Unfortunately Cronus is off-planet. Perhaps Maya can assist.* He rolls his eyes as if expecting an uncomfortable interaction. *Let's go to the Time Chamber.*

"Time Chamber?"

*The Time Stream runs from the Time Chamber in the Temple to innumerable space-time connection points. Although the Galactic Leaders banned time travel, anyone can view the past by using the Time Stream Immersive Projectors scattered throughout the planet's public halls, schools and universities. These have proved invaluable for learning about our own past and for studying other planets, cultures and civilisations.*

"Indeed. I have used those many times."

*Cronus assigned responsibility of the Time Chamber and Immersive Projectors to his daughter.*

"Makes sense."

We walk in silence through enormous high-ceilinged halls. Then into the elevator and down a few levels. The doors open. No crystal walls, no natural light.

"This is different."

*High security. Few are allowed here.*

The ante-chamber scans our energy signatures and demands a password. Guest authorisation is granted.

Above the large stone archway is an embossed inscription: Zakti dAyitva Azaya

*Power. Responsibility. Virtue.*

The last words of Cronus flit across my consciousness. Azaya also translates as 'point' or 'intention'. This beautiful language is part of our ancient culture. As our telepathic abilities progressed, language gradually faded and disappeared. Communication is now mostly via the instant thought-force.

He pauses to view the access logs. A frown creases his brow. *Priya was a recent guest.*

"Galactic Leader Savitri. What are you doing here?"

He looks up and gives a respectful bow. *Maya. Good to see you.*

Hands move to hips. "Well?"

*Investigating a ripple in the time line.*

"Yes, I know about it. It happened a few hours ago. How did you find out?"

*Priya has disappeared from the planet. Hence, Indra is with me.*

"I see." Long pause. "You know she was my guest?"

*Indeed. Care to explain?*

Shrewd. I remain silent.

"She approached me with uncommon information about the operation of the Time Stream. Knowledge way above the average Arcturian. I allowed her access in order to record and test her ideas."

*It is likely that the Time Stream is connected to her disappearance.*

"We can track the incident by using the Immersive Projector. Give me a minute."

Immersion allows you to be present at an event, with the ability to see and hear everything. However, you are an invisible witness; it is impossible to interfere.

I whisper into the galactic leader's ear.

*Find Priya and track recent events in the entertainment sector.*

We watch her frequent visits to the Dark Shop. Always the perspective is from outside.

*Why can't we see inside?*

"I don't know. It's an anomaly."

Again, the finger on thoughtful lips.

*Show events that occurred in the Time Chamber over the last few weeks.*

"That's impossible. For security purposes those time lines can only be viewed from within the Time Stream."

*Who has current access to the Stream?*

"Same as always. Only my father enters the Time Stream."

*And you?*

"My job is on-planet. Under strict instructions."

A diplomat knows when to walk away. If the galactic leader is frustrated, it is masterfully disguised.

"I assure you, Savitri, we will locate the problem and repair it. All will be well."

As she bows, a silver-blue key exposes itself. Hanging on a chain around her neck. I make a mental note: An excellent place to keep a sacred object.

I step forward quickly. "May I?"

Galactic Leader Savitri nods his approval. She sighs reluctantly.

Turning the key in my hand, I find the inscription: 'dve'. I gaze directly into her eyes. "Priya has an identical key, except hers is inscribed with the word 'treeni'."

Maya flushes slightly. She marches across to a large vault. Energy scan. Password. Door opens. After a few minutes she returns. "The third Time Key is missing. It never leaves the vault. My father carries the first key, marked 'ekam'; I carry the second key, marked 'dve'."

*How is that possible?*

She folds her arms. "I don't know. Apart from the Time Lord and his daughter, no one in the galaxy has access to the vault."

*The answer lies within the Time Stream.*

Savitri turns toward the ante-chamber. Maya bounds back to the vault. I quietly tap his shoulder. "I will find that time line. Make it appear as if I left with you."

He bows slightly. *Take care of yourself.*

I walk to the Time Stream and make the leap.

* * *

The usual undulating chaos. I quiet my mind and focus. There is probably a vast amount to learn about Time but at least I am getting the hang of Travel.

Slow down ... visualise my planet ... the Temple ... specify date ... Time Chamber ... a strange red door appears ... push ... will not open ... don't all exits automatically open? ... floating ... how to solve this riddle? ... perhaps this is another high security area ... access only for the Time Lord ... is this an entrance instead of an exit? ... idea flashes ... the keys are not identical ... they are marked for a reason ... different privileges linked to each key ... I have the Time Lord's key!

I insert the key and cross the threshold. A secret room within the Time Stream! Completely and utterly empty, apart from a huge active Immersion reflecting an image of the galaxy. Cool and mysterious.

Setting my intention ... Arcturus ... Mani ... Temple ... Time Chamber ... date ... here we go ... Maya is working ... she is dancing ... exquisite and graceful ... move forward ... vault is open ... catalogue screen ... drawers ... glass receptacles containing peculiar objects ... cubicle and table ... book with Śastra-Vidyā scrawled on the cover, meaning 'weapon-knowledge' ... a strange device comprising a bar with spindles on each end ... labelled as the Vajra ... interesting but not useful.

Take a deep breath ... move forward ... Maya and Priya arriving through the ante-chamber ... heartbreaking ... confusing ... I miss her so much! ... so hard not being able to touch or connect ... need to concentrate on the mission ... hmm, have not seen that ring before ... on Priya's left hand ... large black stone ... is that obsidian? ... generating a close-up ... appears to be obsidian encompassed by fine silver ... rapt conversation ... Maya studiously listening ... walking to the vault ... opens ... oh! ... Priya is dialling her ring ... what the –?

Maya appears frozen ... everything is unmoving ... except for Priya who strolls into the vault and begins systematically searching ... apparently relaxed and unhurried ... eventually finds a cabinet mounted on the back wall ... there's the third key!

*You must be disappointed.*

Startled, I dart out of the Immersion. Distinctive robe. "Cronus!"

*Indeed.*

"I'm sorry. I can explain."

He waves his hand. *No need. You cannot enter Atra Atha without my key.*

"You gave it to me."

*I know.*

"You told me to fix the time line."

*Do you want to understand what happened here?*

I steady myself. "Yes please."

*Your wife has a time-dilation ring. It bends time by creating different velocities.*

"Huh?"

*To simplify, velocity and gravity each slow down time as they increase. In a sense, Maya is functioning in her regular time but Priya is moving extremely fast. However, one can also say that Maya is frozen in time and Priya is moving at her regular pace. Or that Maya is moving normally while Priya is continually looping back in time.*

"Wow."

Brief laughter. *It's all relative.*

Mulling that over in my head. Working with the Cosmic Energy Shield and public policy is one thing but Time is a whole other reality. Being a planetary leader was somewhat less complicated than being a time apprentice.

*The real question is: Where did she get the ring?*

"I have an idea. May I?"

*Go ahead.*

We move into the Immersion. Feel a bit of pressure with the Time Lord standing next to me. This is his domain. What do I know? Come on, get a grip. Focus … backward … entertainment sector … Dark Shop … there … hmm, we are stuck outside again …

*Fascinating and impudent!*

"Excuse me?"

*Who dares hide from the Time Lord?*

I tremble slightly.

A flurry of motion … images flying across the Immersion … time sequences reversing … penetrating the obscure mist … gradually a shadowy figure appears … dressed in a black hooded robe … seldom emerging from his premises … delving further back … searching for the arrival on Mani … no clue in the planetary access logs …

*He couldn't have appeared out of nowhere.*

"Um … after Priya entered his shop, I followed … but everything and everyone had disappeared."

*I wonder …*

Casting my mind back … thick red curtain … that hiss … oh yes …

"Uh … there was a blue light in the shop's back room. I couldn't see because of the curtain and I was concentrating on the peculiar whispering. But I remember the blue light seeping through the gap. There was a time portal."

*Aha.*

Silence. Unmoving. Momentary unease.

"His name is Apep. Sorry, I forgot." That burst out unnaturally. Must be the nerves.

Still nothing. Best to keep still and wait.

Finally … movement …

*Accessed the Universal Index. There was a shape-shifter named Apep but he changed his name to Apophis. Practitioner of the dark arts. His natural form is that of a tall lizard.*

"That's him! The assistant referred to him as the Dark Lizard."

*He belongs to another galaxy.*

"How did he get here? How did he remain hidden?"

*Each galaxy has its own Time Stream. Just as time lines occasionally touch or overlap, the same occurs with the Streams.*

"Okay …"

*A skilful time traveller can cross over at an intersection point. It is inherently risky though.*

"Risky?"

*Time travel is a complicated endeavour. And if you traverse into a new Stream, you have no idea what beings or worlds you will encounter.*

"Why was Apophis hidden from you?"

*He was obviously residing at the intersection point, only maintaining a foothold in our Stream. I cannot see into another galaxy's Stream.*

So, Apophis is a master of time travel in his own galaxy. Is it purely a coincidence that his intersection point gave access to the leadership of another galaxy? Unlikely.

"What about the Time Keys?"

*There are three Time Keys for each Time Stream. Each set of keys belongs to and can only operate within a particular Stream. The master key is held by the Time Lord. The two lesser keys are for the time apprentices. Only the master key can access the secret room hidden in the respective Stream.*

"The Atra Atha room?"

*It's just called Atra Atha.*

"I am guessing that intersection points can only be viewed from Atra Atha or the Time Chamber."

*Indeed. Apophis is either a Time Lord or he has stolen information about intersection points.*

"Power. Responsibility. Virtue. There is no way he is a Time Lord. Most likely he used subterfuge to become a time apprentice. That would explain how he came to possess a time-dilation ring. Even more likely: He found or stole the ring, gained access to his galaxy's Time Chamber, then stole an apprentice's Time Key. He then travelled to the intersection point, seduced the mind of Priya, and got her to steal one of our galaxy's keys in exactly the same manner."

*Wise deduction, young Indra.*

"He now has a key for each galaxy's Time Stream and can travel as he pleases."

*That makes him a very powerful and dangerous being.*

"Where is Priya?"

The Time Lord studies the Immersion, shuffling and moving time sequences. *Her time line ended a few hours ago.*

"What does that mean?"

He looks at me kindly. *Your wife is no longer with us. I'm sorry.*

The last thing I hear is my own anguished scream.

* * *

Swimming through a wall of tears. A cascade of sadness, pain, frustration and anger.

I will get her back. There must be a way to fix everything, a way to restore her life and save my planet. Cronus is with me in this time line. He will know what to do.

After a long while I take a deep breath. "What now?"

*This requires some thought. We each have a master key. A two-pronged attack might be useful.*

"We need to travel back to just before Apophis' arrival at the intersection point."

*Yes, but we cannot alter his time line prior to his arrival because it exists in another Stream.*

"I understand. Nothing we do can prevent his arrival in our galaxy."

*Exactly.*

"We could still save Priya."

*Yes, that is possible.*

He analyses the time lines. *This is the closest date estimation for his first appearance. We need to meet outside the shop exactly one day earlier.*

"Meet? Where are you going?"

*To fetch a weapon of light from the Time Chamber. It's the only way to counteract such a dark force.*

"A weapon? We don't use weapons on Mani."

*You are in charge of the Cosmic Energy Shield?*

"Yes."

*Well, what do you think happens off-planet? Who protects technologically weaker races from exploitation, enslavement or annihilation?*

"The Galactic Military."

*Sometimes peace comes at a price.* His voice sounds jaded by experience. It feels disrespectful to ask about his life.

"I will see you outside the shop at sunrise."

*Perfect.*

We leap into the Time Stream and part ways. A few moments later I find the door and arrive at the destination.

There is no shop. Only a blackened crater. Holding down the panic, I glance along the street. Yep, it's the right place. I run through the scorched rubble. There he is, long coat reduced to rags, blood everywhere.

"Cronus!" I cradle him in my arms. "What happened?"

*He was here when I arrived. Caught me by surprise. Almost as if he was waiting.*

"How can that be?"

*Indra, the mantle passes to you now.*

"What are you saying?"

*Take my necklace. The weapon is called the Vajra. Touch to activate.*

It slinks onto my palm. I'll make sense of his words later.

He looks sternly into my eyes. *Take care of Maya.*

I nod solemnly. He gasps a final breath.

On my knees, rocking back and forth. Clutching my head. What is going on? Cronus has died twice in front of me. Is this some sort of déjà vu? Is it possible to change the future? Is it possible to alter history?

I peruse the necklace. The master key is missing. Frantically search his pockets and the surrounding debris. Wait. Apophis has deliberately changed the time line. He now holds the Time Lord's key and the apprentice's key. Clearly, it is possible to shift reality. Need to get my head together. Think.

Stand up and walk to the street. In the distance, a familiar figure. Priya! She's alive! My heart feels warm. I want to run to her, embrace her, but resist the urge. This is the past. She is still deceased in the future. No need to further complicate the time line. Besides, no time-place is safe with Apophis in our galaxy.

I have this impulse to jump back into the Time Stream and arrive at the Dark Shop a little earlier, so preventing Cronus' death. But the Dark Lizard is cunning and shrewd. He has probably already jumped further into the past. He may be tracing Cronus' time line … he could, in fact, go back and prevent Cronus' birth.

I stop and blink a few times. Does Apophis know about me? Could he be targeting the planetary leaders? Is it he who sabotaged the Cosmic Energy Shield and brought chaos and destruction to our world?

Strolling to the nearest blue portal. Insert the key and make the leap. Then it really hits me. Is Apophis engaging in random acts of violence or is this a well-planned and coordinated attack? Does he have a personal vendetta with Arcturians?

* * *

Floating in the Time Stream. What to do? Where to go? Can I risk returning to Atra Atha? Drifting … turning over various possibilities …

The best course of action is to track Apophis. I need to watch him, learn how he operates, discover his strategy. The hunter needs to become the hunted.

I arrive at the secret room and cautiously peek through the door. Empty. Step inside. Immediately feel the shivers. He was here. Must have just missed him.

The Immersion is still active. I play back the recent viewings. Yes, I was right. He is tracking the planetary leaders. However, his attention seems keenly focused on Cronus. Perhaps he fears reprisal from such a knowledgeable and experienced being. Apophis appears to be stalking the Time Lord.

I gaze at the time line of Cronus. It is far longer than the average Arcturian. Stretching back over thousands of years, it meanders along numerous planets, cultures and civilisations. A divine descendant of Gaia the primordial goddess, he invariably established himself as a respected leader of countries and worlds. Restless and ever-seeking, he accrued titles, wealth and power, but usually moved on after a few decades.

Hmm ... How has he lived for so long? Can he shape-shift? Can he transfer his consciousness? No wonder he is so secretive.

My eyes widen. Apophis is generating a time line. He must have travelled back and started creating a past in our galaxy. Where is he? Aha. Taurus Constellation. Home of the Seven Sisters, an open star cluster. Also known as the Pleiades. On a planet called dUta.

How do I keep up? It's a breathless chase. Should I jump to the same time-place and discreetly follow him? Arcturians look very different to Pleiadeans. I am afraid I would stand out. Does he know how to identify me?

Stop. Close my eyes. Deep breath. Maya is monitoring the Time Stream. She must have witnessed the end of her father's time line. Galactic Leader Savitri would have been notified. The Galactic Military has probably been despatched.

The Time Lord's words flit into my consciousness. Picking up the mantle. Taking responsibility. I suddenly feel so alone. Wish I was back in my world, laying in the warm sunshine with Priya. Perhaps these are the burdens of a time apprentice.

I slip into the Time Stream and find the door for dUta. My first time in the Pleiades. It's going to be an interesting experience.

* * *

I woke up tired this morning. You know that kind of strange empty feeling? Like when you need the touch of someone you love? I feel like that. Some days I just don't want to get out of bed. What is greater than snuggling under the duvet and cuddling someone you love?

The sun is streaming through the white shutters and dancing across the pillows. Arcturians have evolved to the point where we recharge directly from cosmic energy. It is free and abundant. All our planets are shielded, although it is probably more correct to say 'filtered'. Only beneficial energy is allowed to flow in and bathe our worlds. Biological food became an irrelevance long ago. Our planets are pristine and untouched by excavations for primitive energy sources like oil and coal.

Each of us carries a portable energy shield for those rare occasions when we are off-world. This is automatically activated and, apart from assisting our energy requirements, provides a degree of personal protection. I seldom leave my planet. Everything I need is there. Our worlds are supremely peaceful, free of even the slightest traces of poverty, crime and violence. Weapons are banned on all our planets and are only utilised by the Galactic Military.

Yes, it's a sad fact of life. Not all planets in our galaxy are peaceful. The Immersion Projectors reflect deceit, manipulation, inequality, exploitation, poverty and war. I have often wondered about the causes of these terrible conditions. Part of the problem is the limited resources on some planets – scarcity of food, water and energy. Yet, other planets have a sheer abundance that is gathered and hoarded by a privileged and powerful minority. The rich cavort in their sumptuous playgrounds while the poor struggle and suffer. How can such behaviour be condoned?

The Galactic Leaders have debated those issues frequently and in great depth. It's a balancing act. If we expose ourselves and our advanced technology to a relatively primitive race, we run the risk of interfering in their natural spiritual, cultural and global evolution. This has been proved time and time again. 'Interference is Perilous' is the guideline. So, do we stand by and watch races violating each other and damaging their planets? Or do we step in as 'gods and aliens', fostering acquiescence, dependence and fear? Do we really want to start another religion? There is also the possibility that local powers will appropriate our technology to further manipulate and control their fellow beings.

Generally we stay away and observe from a distance. Nothing can replace the autonomy, responsibility and evolution of a people. No doubt this policy leaves some advanced souls more than a little frustrated.

I shift across to the bigger sunbeam. Ah, this is the life. Warm, relaxed and cosy. I think the words in the Time Chamber say it all: Power. Responsibility. Virtue. Too many races on too many planets strive for power, wealth and dominance, while shunning responsibility for fellow beings and their planet. Imagine devastating the world you inhabit purely because of greed and selfishness. Everyone loses in the end. I shake my head. Insane.

To truly embrace spiritual and technological evolution, you need virtue. Integrity, impeccability, loving-kindness, compassion ... those are the gateways to creating a peaceful and joyful world. How much simpler can it get?

Anyway, that's the world I knew and loved. The world I am now trying to save. We are the leaders of the galaxy for good reason. Few beings are more spiritually or technologically advanced than Arcturians.

Reminds me of the reason I am here. Get out of bed, don the hooded cloak. Stare out the window at this blue-tinged world. Quite beautiful. Pleiadeans are mostly the same height as us but more humanoid in appearance. A very gentle and peaceful race, they are steadily catching up to our level of knowledge and wisdom. They are trustworthy allies in the Galactic Federation.

It seems I am still on my own. The Galactic Military never arrived. Perhaps they were not informed of the threat. I wonder what Maya is doing.

Off to Apophis' last known location. He appears to be infiltrating the GenLabs on this planet. The records show that Pleiadeans are hard at work analysing, testing and perfecting biological systems. Genetic engineering, also called genetic modification, is the direct manipulation of an organism's genome (hereditary information encoded in DNA or RNA) using biotechnology. This mostly involves the insertion of new DNA into the host genome; it may also include the removal, addition or mutation of existing genes.

It's like chasing a ghost. How does he get around so easily? Yes, he is a shape-shifter ... still ... Does he have a base of operations on this planet? Is he collecting samples and data to take back to his own lab, or is he simply working right under the noses of local scientists and technicians?

Another unsuccessful day. Faint shivers indicate his recent presence outside one or two labs. People report unusual activity near a genetic storage facility. Why am I constantly arriving too late? He is always a few steps ahead, seemingly just out of reach.

Two months have gone by. My frustration is increasing. Every morning feels the same. Does the angle of that sunbeam ever change? Why does Apophis adopt an identical daily routine? I gaze out the window. That couple always walks past my apartment at this exact time ... hmm ... so do they ... and that vehicle ...

Oh. Is this the same day happening over and over? No, it can't be!

I leap into the Time Stream and enter the secret room. It's always a risk coming here. Walk into the Immersion, gather the relevant time lines and place them alongside each other. Shake off the shiny black dust. There! Apophis is on the move. Using a time door at this very moment. Drop everything, rush into the undulating waves, visualise –

"Indra, stop!"

"Maya, what are you doing here?"

"My father's time line ended. I tracked the event and saw you. You are chasing a very powerful and devious Reptilian."

"He's just left the Time Stream. We can catch him."

"Was there any obsidian dust?"

"What?"

"Shiny black dust?"

"Uh … yeah …"

"If you go through that door, you will enter a time loop."

"A what?"

She looks at me calmly. "Time will repeat indefinitely. You will be trapped in a recurring set of events."

"Oh." I feel a bit embarrassed.

"Have you got a key to Atra Atha?"

"Yes. Your father gave it to me. It's a long story."

"Thought as much. Come on. Let's go."

I explain the origin of my journey, the demise of our planet, the déjà vu with her father, and the resultant chase through time.

"An onerous mantle. He must have chosen you for a reason."

I shrug. "No idea what I am doing."

"You'll get the hang of it."

We step into the secret room. She pulls a silver amulet from her necklace and blows through it. Tiny shimmering flakes flutter into the Immersion.

"Amulet of Clarity."

"Huh?"

"A sacred object. Worth collecting."

I nod. Maybe it will make sense later.

She gathers the time lines. "My, my … he has been busy … that's a compact history. Do you know if he has a time-dilation ring?"

"He does."

"While you were stuck in the time loop, he spent the equivalent of one year on dUta."

I cough softly. "An entire year?"

"Yep. He is way ahead of us."

I glance at the time line. DNA sequencing. Experimentation. It's all visible now. "What is he planning?"

"Building an army, no doubt."

She sounds as jaded and experienced as her father. Maya is an Arcturian name; it means 'illusion'. I wonder if she is a true Arcturian or if she has a long and eventful history like Cronus.

"Help me sift through the Immersion. We need to gather as much information as possible."

Relieved to prove myself at least moderately useful, I grab a few time lines and get to work.

"A challenging adversary. It is now my personal mission to avenge my father."

Wow. Arcturians don't really do vengeance.

I heave a sigh. Tomorrow is probably going to be another long day.

* * *

And then it happens. Right in front of us. The Time Stream wobbles.

Maya points at a quivering time line. "Apophis is on the move. That audacious lizard has stolen a small spacecraft. He appears to have a number of entities with him."

"What are we going to do?"

"Chase him!"

"Why is the Time Stream wobbling?"

"The rule is: One key, one traveller. Unless you have a time-adapted ship. He has forced a spacecraft with occupants into the Stream. How many keys does he have?"

"One master key from Cronus and the apprentice's key that Priya gave him. And a key from his own galaxy."

"That last one is irrelevant. He cannot use another galaxy's key in our Stream. He has probably attempted to adapt the spacecraft. Only the Time Lord can programme a key for such use. Whichever key he uses in the ship, it will quickly self-destruct."

"Oh."

She looks at me impatiently. "Come on!"

Rush to our home planet. Board her personal spacecraft. Glowing, highly reflective and disc-shaped, it is beautiful and magical to behold. The ship is operated almost entirely by thought, requiring only a modicum of manual control. Maya graces the captain's chair and inserts her Time Key into a luminous blue panel. Never seen that on any other ship.

Noticing my captivation, she smiles briefly. "It has been modified for time travel. Observe the console screen. I have isolated the time line. Navigate us to chase Apophis."

Whoa. In the deep end. Focus my mind … lock on the time line … visualise … concentrate … We make the jump. A burst of brilliant light. Shimmers of streaking white, as if we are surrounded by a billion shooting stars.

"My father built this ship. It was crafted and honed using his vast knowledge and experience."

"As a Time Lord?"

"Yep. And as a seasoned warrior."

"Oh." My trepidation increases slightly.

"You have seen battle before?"

Raising my open hands. "I am just a regular Arcturian. Grew up on a peaceful world. Conflict is foreign to me."

"Soft-bellied planetary leaders … No wonder it ends up a mess."

Ouch.

I glance at the screen. Our ship is fast. Closing in rapidly … just ahead … another silvery reflective disc.

"It's a common design. Highly functional. Spinning outside, static centre, advanced magnetic and anti-gravity instrumentation.

The flat shape and rapid spin counteract various forces, some of which flow relatively unhindered over the ship."

"Aha."

"He's heading toward planet Earth."

My face grimaces. "Primitive aggressive people."

She smiles like she knows a secret. "They're not all bad."

Suddenly a dark beam streaks across and deflects off our ship. Then another and another.

I swallow hard. "Are we in danger?"

"Not at all. Our ship is far superior. But firing in the Time Stream is incredibly stupid and dangerous."

"Why?"

"You cannot control the deflections. Unpredictable."

A boom shakes our craft. Maya stabilises it quickly. "That's exactly what I feared."

Apophis' ship has burst into flame. It rebounds sharply then ricochets out of the Time Stream.

She rolls her eyes. "Check the time-place. Navigate."

I hurriedly scrutinise the screen. Planet Earth. New Mexico. Local date: July 7, 1947.

We exit the Time Stream and follow the blazing trail. There's a terrible crash and resounding explosion.

Hovering invisibly, 40 metres above the site. No movement below. The screen shows our location: A sheep ranch close to a town called Roswell. Two humans on horseback soon appear; the older male stands still for a long while then slowly inspects the huge trench and surrounding debris. He slips a few pieces of metal into his saddlebag. The child remains with his horse, surreptitiously retrieving one small object that lies nearby.

Maya sighs. "That is precisely why time travel was banned. Consider the fallout and potential time ripples."

It's a judgement call. "Should we interfere?"

"Not yet. Scan all life forms."

Yay. I am useful again. "Um … two humans … older male's energy signature recorded as William Brazel … unrelated child … and six small beings, each approximately 1.2 metres tall (4 feet in ancient measurement), no identity on record … three of those beings are dead …"

"Where is Apophis?"

"I cannot see him."

We immediately begin scouring a vast area. The screen shows that Apophis is definitely in this time-place. Maya is intent on finding him. I am more concerned with what's happening at the crash site. Several hours later and no luck.

It's now quite busy on the ground. Members of the Sheriff's Office and the Roswell Army Air Field are scattered across an area almost a kilometre long. Trucks are arriving. A civilian is furiously taking notes; he promptly gets into a vehicle and hurriedly drives away. It's out of our control. No choice but to hover and wait.

Sheriff George Wilcox and RAAF Major Jesse Marcel are supervising the transport of the alien bodies. The strange grey beings offer no resistance. Three are placed in body bags while the other three are carried to one of the smaller trucks. Gradually every piece of evidence is collected and removed from the site.

Maya studies the locale. "Alright. This is good. Minimal exposure to the public. We can salvage the situation."

"How?" As the words leave my mouth, I already know the answer.

"You need to mingle with the witnesses and cloud their minds. It's the only way to prevent a serious ripple in the time line."

"Maya, I have an Arcturian body."

She leans forward, exposing her dazzling necklace. It's full of shiny trinkets. "You really have some catching up to do." She laughs gleefully. "Fortunately, I have two of these ..."

I open my palm and scrutinise the gleaming silver object.

"Unfold it and place around your wrist. Then command the image you desire."

"It's telekinetic?"

"Of course."

"Will I shape-shift?"

"No. It projects an image so you can blend into the populace."

Hmm ... primitive aggressive unequal societies ... go with masculine ... pale skin ... severe black suit ... ah, Counter Intelligence Corps ... that will work ...

"You forgot the hair."

Oh yeah ... how weird ... short dark hair ... black hat ... "How's that?"

"Perfect. Remember, you cannot see your image. The only way you know it's working is by the reaction of others."

"Seriously?"

"Yes. And by the bracelet. If that green stone is lit up, you're safe."

"You silly joker."

"Good luck."

"Where are you going?"

"One of us has to stay with the ship and search for Apophis."

"Oh yeah ..."

I am beamed to the ground in less than a second.

***

A short walk to the waiting trucks. I sift through the wreckage and quickly locate the master console. Yep, Maya was right – a melted key. Only a tiny piece of the blade remains. I can barely make out three letters 'tre'. Apophis has destroyed the apprentice's key.

Next stop, the ranch. A brief conversation with a military airman and I have a chauffeur and vehicle at my disposal. It is relatively easy to locate William Brazel and those connected to him. I am kindly invited to dinner, providing a perfect pretext to cloud the minds of the family.

We travel to Roswell in the morning. It is July 8. The airman gives me a copy of the Roswell Daily Record. The newspaper headline reads: RAAF Captures Flying Saucer On Ranch In Roswell

Region. Time to step up the pace. We swing by two radio stations and the newspaper building for a quiet chat. Then it's a brief visit at the Sheriff's Office. Finally we make our way to the military base to meet Colonel William Blanchard, Major Jesse Marcel and Lieutenant Walter Haut (RAAF public information officer).

In the evening I go in search of the mysterious bodies. Three of them are in the RAAF morgue. Glenn Dennis, a young civilian mortician, is being escorted off the premises. It takes just a minute to modify his memories. Mind clouding is meant to be a short-term defensive strategy, something not required on my home world. Never understood why Galactic Leader Savitri taught me this military technique. I wonder if the effects are permanent.

Two of the grey beings are lying unconscious in the hospital. A couple of armed guards stand outside the room while an authorised doctor and nurse conduct an inspection. I glance at my bracelet. The green stone is shining. Throwing out a general mind cloud. Approaching the peculiar beings. The skin is greyish and wet. Large black eyes (though not as large as mine), tiny nose and mouth. Probing its consciousness ... there's Apophis in a lab ... long black hooded robe ... can't see his face ... clone experiments ... belong to the Dark Lizard ... unquestioning loyalty ... distraction so Apophis can steal a spacecraft ... five grey beings on board ... names of these two survivors ... Sek and Mot ...

The being blinks and opens its eyes. I jump back, startled, and the connection is broken. Retreating to the doorway, I catch a snippet of the guards' conversation: "... moving the alien bodies to Fort Worth Army Air Field in Texas ... tomorrow ... jurisdiction of Brigadier General Ramey, commanding officer of the 8th Air Force ..." Hmm, that's the state just east of New Mexico. Hope Maya is tracking my movements.

The next morning, July 9, the Roswell Daily Record carries a very different headline: General Ramey Empties Roswell Saucer. The article explains that the crashed object was actually a weather balloon and denounces the flying saucer story as implausible nonsense. How interesting. General Ramey has started a disinformation campaign. Who spoke to him? Who got to him before me?

I board the transport plane with the five alien bodies. The being called Sek is observing me closely. Slightly unnerved, I compulsively check my bracelet. Everything seems fine. Fortunately the aliens are all restrained. Who knows their capabilities? A thought makes my skin tingle: Where is the sixth alien from the crash site?

Disembarking … check the base map … this way to the General's office. The moment I enter, those familiar shivers cascade through me. Apophis! How did he get here first? That cunning lizard went straight to the top of the command chain. What did he tell the General? Oh … that is why the alien debris and bodies were transported here. Apophis plans to reunite with his clones. Does he still carry the technology and data from the Pleiades?

I am now at a serious disadvantage. Apophis is here but has obviously shape-shifted. How will I identify him? My eyes widen. He was the sixth alien! Right under our noses all along. Probably shifted his form into a military person as soon as the bodies were extracted from the craft. Worked out the hierarchy and went straight to Texas. I bite my lip and frown. Two steps behind, again.

What is his strategy? Clearly, we are both encouraging the suppression of information. However, I am trying to protect this planet's time line. Casting my mind back … the words of Cronus … ah, yes … Apophis is a practitioner of the dark arts. So here's the profile: Power-hungry, destructive, ignores all rules … values no life but his own … or perhaps he does not value Life …

The people of Earth are highly resistant to tyranny and terror. Apophis would have done his research. The only way to gain power is through subterfuge and illusion. Allow the people to believe they are free, that they have choices, while encasing them in an invisible prison. To do this, he would need to control the purveyors of ideology: education, religion, mass media.

Wow. What's happening to me? Am I thinking like a strategist? Perhaps Maya was right ... this soft-bellied leader needs to wise up. We are not on Arcturus anymore.

Apophis will ensure that his true goals remain hidden. The general public will never learn about the existence of extraterrestrial life. That is no longer my problem. It's time for a new mission: Track and incapacitate the Dark Lizard. For the sake of all our worlds. I have to smile. That sounds very much like Maya.

Working alone is no longer beneficial. I need to infiltrate this country's government and warn them of the impending threat, while somehow managing potential disruptions in the time line. Checking the flight schedule in the General's office. A military plane is leaving for the nation's capital in an hour. I'll make sure I am on it.

A subtle mind-probe yields some interesting facts from a fellow passenger. Washington D.C. is the capital of the United States of America. Its official name is the District of Columbia; however, it is informally referred to as Washington, the District or simply D.C. The U.S. Constitution permits the District to be under the exclusive jurisdiction of the Congress; it is therefore not part of any U.S. state. The surrounding states of Maryland and Virginia each donated land to form the federal district. The District hosts the centres of the legislative, executive and judiciary branches of the federal government, including the Congress, President and Supreme Court.

The Congress is the legislative body and comprises the House of Representatives and the Senate. Democratic elections result in the appointment of representatives (two-year term) and senators (six-year term) from the various states. The President resides at the White House.

A stranger in a strange land. Where do I start making connections?

The United States Botanic Garden in D.C. has a strong appeal. It presents an opportunity to take a break from the constant chase. I meander along diverse flowers and plants, savouring the rich scents of nature, then flit into the delightful butterfly garden. Passing the Conservatory, I cross Independence Avenue and discover beautiful Bartholdi Park with its family of trees, shrubs, vines and roses. The centrepiece of the park is the Fountain of Light and Water. I relax on a secluded bench, catching glimmers of the late afternoon sun. Magnificent ... reminds me of home ...

A well-dressed gentleman is strolling up the path. He catches the attention of passers-by immediately. Acknowledges every person with a nod and broad smile. Charismatic. Interesting. Probably someone important. Having no knowledge of the local protocols, I ignore him. This seems to have the reverse effect and he sits down next to me.

"Do you mind?" His grey-green eyes flash at me.

"Not at all. There's plenty of space."

Slowly unwraps a brown elongated object and cuts off the end. The small red label reads: H.Upmann/Habana/Cuba. Extracts a silver device and applies a flame. Soon puffs of smoke waft around his reddish-brown hair. How peculiar.

"You're not from around here, are you?"

I shake my head.

"John Fitzgerald Kennedy, House of Representatives, at your service."

"Ah, the Congress. You are a political leader."

"Yep. Six months in office. Long way to go."

He explains his political leaning – moderately conservative Democrat – and outlines some of the challenging issues of the day.

I nod appreciatively. A thought flutters across my mind.

"What do you think about the Roswell incident?"

He removes his hat and rubs his forehead. "Can't stand these things. Why do people wear them?" Brief pause. "Are you a reporter?"

"No. I am a leader in my world."

Penetrating gaze. "They recovered a flying disc. Rest of the story is a cover-up. Would love to get to the bottom of it."

"That crash brought imminent danger to your planet."

"Who are you? Don't think you introduced yourself."

The energy emanating from this man reflects integrity and honesty. And a deeply curious nature. I extend my hand while looking directly into his eyes. "Are you a virtuous man, John Fitzgerald Kennedy?"

A sincere smile. "Surely."

"I am Indra, a planetary leader on Mani. A blue-green jewel orbiting the star Arcturus."

Stillness settles. The silent scramble for appropriate words.

"It's probably best that you see my true form. Prepare to be astonished."

Briefly survey the area to ensure we are alone. Deactivate the bracelet. The shining stone dulls. Image fades instantly.

Unflinching. Speechless. Taking it all in. Eventually a slow puff of smoke and subdued whisper: "Always wondered ..."

I reactivate the projection. "You wish to continue the conversation?"

He gets to his feet and stretches. "Let's go for a walk."

We amble along Pennsylvania Avenue toward President's Park (which is adjacent to the White House complex).

"I have so many questions."

"Using your perspective: Arcturus of the Boötes constellation is the brightest star in the northern celestial hemisphere, located approximately thirty-six light years from Earth. It is the fourth brightest star in the night sky, after Sirius, Canopus and Alpha Centauri. Arcturus is about 180 times more luminous than your sun."

He escorts me around the Ellipse then across the park to the Washington Monument. A proud wave of the hand. "That monument is made of marble, granite and bluestone gneiss. It is both the world's tallest stone structure and the world's tallest obelisk at 555 feet."

Hmm, that's 169 metres. "Impressive."

We glance at each other and burst into ebullient laughter.

"Can you stay for a few weeks?"

"It will be my honour."

Twilight casts long shadows across the grass. An image of a black hooded robe flutters across my consciousness. I shiver involuntarily. It's time to strike into the heart of my enemy.

* * *

The next month is a melange of pleasant walks and deep discussions amid the hurly-burly of a politician's life. He is a very interesting man. Huge heart ... deeply concerned about civil rights ... visionary ... wanting to bring about positive change ... committed to honest transparent government ... a true man of the people. His youthful appearance and relaxed informal style seem to irk some of the older members of the Washington establishment. This 30-year-old sure has some challenges ahead of him.

We are sitting on the bench where we first met. I am getting used to the strange cigars, even though polluting one's own lungs makes no sense to me. Humans have such short lifespans. Perhaps one day they will grasp the value of their bodies.

He leans across and whispers: "Tell me about the fifth dimension again."

Take a deep breath. Think back to my childhood lessons.

"What is 5D?

"Zero dimension or 0D is called a singularity. Try to imagine a dimensionless fixed point, a bit like using a pencil to make a dot on a page.

"Now imagine drawing a straight line from that dot. That is one dimension or 1D. If you draw another line extending from the dot at a 90-degree angle from the first line, you have two dimensions or 2D."

I take out a piece of paper and lay it on the bench.

"This is a simplified example of 2D: A flat piece of paper with length and breadth. A being living in a 2D world is unable to see beings of a 3D world, although the 2D being might perceive a vague or distorted hint of the 3D beings. The third dimension is the world of planet Earth, the world you know. Length, breadth and depth. Moving from 2D to 3D, a square becomes a cube, a circle becomes an orb, a triangle becomes a pyramid."

He nods. "I am with you so far."

"Time is the fourth dimension. When 3D objects move along a fixed line – past to future – it is called 4D. So technically you live in a 4D world. In the fourth dimension, time appears to move in a single direction. Try to imagine an arrow representing time.

"In 5D an extra dimension of time is added. Time no longer moves in one direction only; it is multi-directional. In your 4D world you can move forward and backward in space; in a 5D world you can move forward and backward in time."

Using a pen, I draw a line across the middle of the blank page. Point A marks the start of the line and point B marks the end of the line.

"Look at this line. To travel from point A to point B involves movement across space and a certain amount of time. Is there a way to move instantly from A to B?"

He stares blankly at the drawing. After a few minutes I fold the paper so that point A is touching point B. "There you go. Instant travel."

John frowns. "Now you lost me."

I sigh. "You only know three spatial dimensions and one time dimension. The fifth dimension is actually the space-time fabric. Similar to folding that page, we can bend the fabric of space-time. Arcturians are able to take a shortcut in the fifth dimension to travel through space and time. It's like a tearing a doorway in the fabric of your reality."

He smiles. "Great analogy. I understand."

"Time travel is fascinating but fraught with potential dangers, inconsistencies and paradoxes. Hence it was banned by the Galactic Leaders. Only the Time Lord of each galaxy travels the Time Stream."

"Are you referring to the dangers introduced by the Roswell crash?"

"Indeed."

"Apophis has yet to surface. Though, to be honest, no one would be able to identify him. As for those aliens, they are firmly under military lock-and-key. Thorough autopsies of the three dead aliens have been completed. Scientists are analysing and cataloguing their remains. The two live ones have been remarkably cooperative, sharing advanced technological and aeronautical information. We have even named their race."

"What are you calling them?"

"Greys. It's short for grey aliens."

"Hmm, catchy name."

John throws his hat into a shrub and laughs. "You worry too much. Imagine the leaps we will make in the next few years."

"You mean in eradicating poverty, disease, inequality, violence and war?"

He shrugs nonchalantly. "Yeah, that too."

I shake my head. "The real danger is a people who advance faster technologically than they do spiritually. Would you like to know the code of the Time Lord?"

"Tell me."

"Power. Responsibility. Virtue. It's worth pondering."

I gaze at the sculptures posing in the Fountain of Light and Water. Sprinkles of sunlight waltz through the dancing streams, creating gently rippling rainbows. A soft breeze rustles the surrounding leaves, coolly counterpointing the *ka ka kow kow* of a Yellow-billed Cuckoo.

After a while: "What did you mean by 'inconsistencies and paradoxes'?"

"Imagine you travel to the past and meet your grandfather. You convince him to take a vacation at the very time he would have met your grandmother. As a result, they never get married and you are never born. If you are never born, you could not have travelled back from the future and met your grandfather."

Broad smile. "A great dinner party conversation-starter."

"The multi-directional nature of time in a 5D world also begs the question of causality. Where is the cause of an effect – in the past or the future? What exactly are the past and the future? Do they even exist?"

"Wow. That's a tough one." He walks over to the shrub and retrieves his hat. "Makes you wonder if there really is such a thing as Time."

I burst into laughter. "You mean everything is Here Now?"

"You should have a chat with physicist Albert Einstein. He became an American citizen in 1940 and currently works at the Institute of Advanced Study in Princeton, New Jersey. It's the state just east of here."

It's my turn to stand and stretch. "Noted."

He dons his hat and stubs out the cigar. "I need to get back to the office. See you later."

Suits me. I wander over to the Conservatory, find the undulating blue door and slip into the Time Stream. There are a few things I need to check.

* * *

First thing: Where is Maya? What is she doing?

I locate her time line. She is reconnoitring the nearby states. Does that mean Apophis is on the move? How does she hope to find him? If she does, what then? Will she simply blast him from the sky?

The two Greys are now registered in the Time Stream. Still present in Texas; nothing much happening. Evidently they carry advanced knowledge in various fields, including genetics, technology and aeronautics. I wonder if the information originated from Apophis or if it was unintentionally inherited from the Pleiadeans. The Greys are lab-created clones which means they are unable to reproduce. Is that why they are so docile? Are they dependent on Apophis? Do they view him as creator and father? Do they even have free will?

I can learn more by moving forward in time and observing the developments. My brief interaction with Maya has shown me a solitary, fiercely independent operator. She won't even miss me. Now, where is JFK's time line?

Catching the fleeting images. Mr Kennedy serves three terms in the House of Representatives before being elected as a Senator. Auspicious moment … setting my intention … blue portal appears … I arrive on Earth in October 1955 and amble across to Bartholdi Park in D.C. A couple of days later a familiar figure comes strolling along. He looks shocked when he sees me.

"Indra! Where have you been? What happened to you?"

I smile warmly. "Saw you a few minutes ago, John."

"You did?"

"Of course. For you, it has been 8 years. For me, we only just said goodbye."

"Really? You time-jumped?"

I nod my head. "Yeah."

"Wow."

"Your political progress is impressive."

"Thank you."

"What else has happened in your world?"

He raises his eyebrows, takes a deep breath and plants himself firmly on the wooden bench. "Where do I start? The most significant event … married the wonderful Jacqueline Lee Bouvier on the morning of September 12, 1953, in Newport, Rhode Island … more than eight hundred guests … hang on, let me show you a picture …"

I gaze at the black-and-white. "Where are all the hats? When I left almost every man was wearing one."

Satisfied grin. "I gave up that social convention long ago. Must have started a trend."

"What's next to go? Those weird pieces of material worn around the neck?"

"You mean ties?"

"Uh huh."

We fall into unrestrained laughter.

I pat his shoulder. "So, tell me about the Greys."

He heaves a sigh. "First off, Einstein passed away a few months ago. A sad loss for our world. Bizarrely, and without permission, the pathologist removed Einstein's brain during the autopsy. His body was cremated but the brain is being preserved for neuro-analysis. Must have been a cold day when I met the pathologist. Got the shivers."

I perk up immediately. "You did?"

"Secondly, Fort Worth Army Air Field was renamed Carswell Air Force Base in February 1948. The Greys were only there a short time. They were subsequently transferred along with the spacecraft debris to Wright-Patterson Air Force Base, Ohio. And they were recently moved again."

"Where are they now?"

"You'll need the backstory. Chapter one. The Central Intelligence Agency is an important intelligence-gathering agency belonging to the United States federal government. The CIA was established in September 1947 and is headquartered in Langley, Virginia, a few miles west of Washington D.C.

"Chapter two. In 1912 two brothers formed the Lockheed aircraft company, completing a maiden voyage in their own flying machine in 1913. Thirty years later, in 1943, the U.S. Army Air Corps commissioned Lockheed to build a new jet fighter. And so was born the top secret high-performing Lockheed Skunk Works division. A decade after that, the renamed United States Air Force sought the construction of a high altitude reconnaissance aircraft. Approval was given in November 1954 for a covertly funded joint USAF-CIA project. Lockheed was awarded the contract in early 1955 and completed the U2 plane in July 1955."

I shrug and stare at the red and yellow leaves falling softly onto the grass. "Not sure I see the connection."

"Wait, here comes the juicy part. The CIA and Lockheed determined that the flight test and pilot training programmes needed to be conducted in extreme secrecy at a remote location. In April 1955 they found Groom Lake, situated in the southern portion of the state of Nevada. The dry flat lakebed provided ideal landing areas and the surrounding mountain ranges offered protection and seclusion. The CIA asked the Atomic Energy Commission to acquire the land which was designated Area 51 on the map.

"Under the direction of Skunk Works, construction began immediately. The new runway, hangars, control tower, mess hall and accommodation were completed by July 1955. The name Area 51 was changed to Paradise Ranch to make it sound more appealing to CIA, Lockheed and USAF personnel. The U2 plane, nicknamed Dragon Lady, arrived and was test flown in early August. Executive Order 10633 was signed by President Eisenhower on 19 August, restricting the airspace over Groom Lake for the first time."

John takes a deep breath. "The Greys were moved to Paradise Ranch two weeks ago, presumably to facilitate aeronautical research and development. They are still remarkably cooperative and pose no perceivable threat."

I scratch my head. "Don't understand it. Where is Apophis? Why is there no imminent danger to your planet? My planet was destroyed."

He looks at me kindly. "You'll work it out."

"I am going to time-jump again. There is little I can offer at the moment. Make you a deal: Let's meet at the Washington Monument in President's Park on November 21, 1960."

"Why that date?"

"Why not?"

"This is so weird. Alright, see you then."

I stroll back to the Conservatory and leap into the Time Stream. It gives me the opportunity to have a good ponder.

Floating among the undulating waves and turning over the possibilities. Apophis has been in one time-place for too long. Is it possible he has lost the Time Key? That would explain his ongoing presence on Earth. In effect, he would be trapped on a planet with severely limited technology and no means of escape.

Hmm ... it makes sense ... he has probably infiltrated academic and military establishments in a desperate attempt to advance their knowledge and information systems. Ah ... that is why the Greys are so cooperative. They are trying to hurry aeronautical development on this planet.

I smile contentedly. It must be tremendously frustrating for the Dark Lizard.

If my theory is correct, then where is the master key? As a time apprentice it is my responsibility to locate it. Apophis could only have lost it during the horrendous crash in 1947. I think back to the subsequent events. That rancher ... and the boy who never left his horse ... didn't he pick up something? Every bit of crash debris was confiscated by the military. Although it was initially shifted to Fort Worth it is now securely stored at Area 51. Apophis would have had ample opportunity to search the debris so there is no point following his path. But the boy ... quite possibly he never found out ...

I find the sheep rancher's time line and follow their movements ... he is the neighbour's son, Dee Proctor ... not present at the mind-clouding dinner at Brazel's house ... move a few days along the time line … ah, there it is! … rolling it in his hand … yep … 'ekam' is written on the blade … move one day forward … key is being placed in his pocket … wait until he is near a glowing door … swoop in and have a chat … job done … two master keys now on my necklace.

Back in the Time Stream. Just realised … by grabbing Apophis' key I have interfered in the time line of Earth. Am I now the one who has trapped the Dark Lizard on this planet? This time stuff boggles my mind. Wish Cronus had taught me more. How can I not interfere? I am trying to save my beloved planet from annihilation.

It's not worth berating myself. I know so little about Time. Best to park those befuddled thoughts and focus on my next appointment. Time-place: Washington Monument, November 21, 1960. I visualise it and make the jump.

***

There he is, right on time. The jubilant figure strolls over and places his hand on my shoulder. "So good to see you! Heard the news?"

Sheepish grin. "No. I've been busy."

"I won the presidential election two weeks ago. I'm now in the position to make some serious changes."

"Congratulations. Amazing achievement. Explains your entourage."

"Don't mind them. Did you solve your problem?"

"Yes. Apophis and the Greys are unable to leave Earth. They are cooperating with your military to enable a means of escape. Hence, no threat."

"That's understandable. Listen, before you disappear again, I have a proposal: Spend the next four years working with me. I could use your wisdom to shape our country and we can search for Apophis together."

The air is chilly and leaves are falling once more. The autumnal colours are magnificent. I consider his offer for a few moments. Positive input from an Arcturian could pre-empt or counteract the destructive actions of a Reptilian. Interference may be perilous but abstinence may be foolish.

I nod. "Alright, let's do it."

He smiles. "Come this way. I want you to meet some people." Then a whisper, "What do I call you?"

Introductions all round. Bodyguards, aides, staffers. As for me, I now have an Earth designation: Indra Black (on account of my dark suit), Technology Consultant.

A politician at this level has a hectic life. We are shunted from meeting to lobby group to policy discussion. The presidential inauguration is just a few weeks away. When it finally arrives on January 20, 1961, it is a momentous occasion. John Fitzgerald Kennedy is sworn in as the 35th president of the United States; at only 43 years old he is the youngest person ever to hold that office. His inaugural address is truly memorable, calling for Americans to work together in the pursuit of progress and the elimination of poverty. The line "Ask not what your country can do for you; ask what you can do for your country" galvanises the public consciousness. He also appeals to the nations of the world to fight together against the "common enemies of man: tyranny, poverty, disease, and war itself" then adding "All this will not be finished in the first one hundred days. Nor will it be finished in the first one thousand days, nor in the life of this Administration, nor even perhaps in our lifetime on this planet. But let us begin."

I wonder if my stories about life on Mani have inspired him. Irrespective, John Fitzgerald Kennedy is a man who has firmly grasped and shouldered the principles of Power, Responsibility and Virtue. I feel kind of proud.

It is another week before the president manages to carve out some breathing space. We take a walk through the park and he catches me up.

"The Greys are still ensconced at the Ranch. Rapid technological and aeronautical advancements are being made, along with major leaps in information and data processing. We'll probably leak the basic computing systems into corporations and educational establishments later in the decade. Project 51 was authorised in October 1960, commencing a multi-year upgrade and extension of Area 51. We are building new runways, hangars, housing and base facilities, including a specialised research and development centre. The restricted airspace directly over Groom Lake will soon be expanded to 22 by 20 nautical miles. Also, Lockheed is now working closely with the National Aeronautics and Space Administration (NASA)."

I shake my head. "Wow. Throw a couple of Greys in the mix and look what happens."

As the weeks go by, my comfort level decreases. I should be doing more to prevent the demise of my planet but am unsure how to proceed. The Greys are clearly not a threat. Although they are creating a ripple in Earth's time line, at least it is a positive one. Apophis is practically invisible, no doubt constantly shifting into different disguises and personas. If he still has the time-dilation ring then I may as well throw my hands up and surrender.

It is obvious that he is working at Paradise Ranch. However, he is probably also scouring the planet in search of materials and technology. Experience has taught me that he is constantly on the move, the modus operandi of a mistrustful, devious and cunning being.

I am reluctant to go to Area 51. I don't believe the answers are lying there. Besides, that brief interaction with Sek the Grey unnerved me. For him, it was 14 years ago; for me, it was very recent. It felt like he was able to penetrate my consciousness, just as I was penetrating his; fortunately he was not in good condition. Meeting them again might expose my true identity, threaten my presence on this planet and possibly jeopardise my relationship with JFK. I need to proceed with caution.

Roaming around the White House. As one of his first presidential acts, Kennedy instructs Congress to create the Peace Corps. So from 1961 thousands of Americans volunteer to help underdeveloped nations in areas such as education, health care, farming and construction. It's an altruistic initiative that warms my heart.

On April 12, 1961, Soviet cosmonaut Yuri Gagarin becomes the first person to fly in space. Russia refuses any international cooperation regarding space exploration (an ironic American request considering the developments at Area 51), raising concerns in the White House about national security. Shortly thereafter I am invited to attend a meeting of the military leaders. John, who now insists that I call him by his nickname Jack, introduces me. Curt respectful greetings all round. A tall lean civilian with cropped white hair extends his hand. Those familiar light blue eyes study mine. *Cronus, Strategic Military Consultant. Have we met before?*

I wonder silently. Is this man from the future? Or is this one of his many incarnations? Is he already connected to Time? Does he know that he will become the Time Lord?

"Good to meet you." I deliberately bow, which serves the purpose of avoiding his hand and causing the Vajra and two keys on my necklace to be exposed. Nothing registers on his face. Hmm ... disguised experience or innocence? Either way, a covert conversation has commenced.

Jack asks me to join Project Space Race. It is the beginning of much deliberation and many vociferous meetings. Finally, in a speech to a Joint Session of Congress on May 25, 1961, the president announces "... I believe that this nation should commit itself to achieving the goal, before this decade is out, of landing a man on the Moon and returning him safely to the Earth."

The project allows me to spend a fair amount of time with Cronus. He proves to be a virtuous and trustworthy person. After a few months I decide to take a gamble and enlist his help. One afternoon, after a long discussion about ethics and advanced weapons development, I look him directly in the eyes and state calmly: "We do know each other. You have lived many lifetimes across diverse planets, cultures and civilisations. Somehow our energy is connected. I met you thousands of years in your future."

He grabs my arm and escorts me out the building. We take a walk down Pennsylvania Avenue toward Bartholdi Park. *Never speak of such things where you can be overheard. It is not our place to influence or corrupt the natural evolution.*

"Way too late for that, I'm afraid. You really don't know ..."

*Know what?*

Standing at the butterfly garden I tell him about Arcturus, the destruction of Mani, his daughter Maya, Apophis, his own death – twice, the threat of time ripples, and the wondrous Time Stream. My temples are throbbing uncomfortably. I have probably broken every rule of Time.

"Anyway, it's easier if I just show you."

Pulling both keys from my necklace. Press one into his palm. Indicate the glowing blue door. Oh yeah ... to him it will appear as an ordinary door. "Insert the key, turn it left, make the leap."

Maybe it's my trustworthy face, maybe it's his inquisitive nature, but he does exactly what I request. Momentary shock … reorientation … big smile. *Whoo hoo! Such power! Even better than being a king!*

"You were once a king?"

*Yep, many times.* Sadness flits across his face.

"Not all happy memories?"

Deep sigh. *A long history includes plentiful triumphs and tragedies. Numerous battle scars, mostly spiritual.*

"Spiritual?"

*I can transfer my consciousness when death is imminent. The scars are not physical. Can you imagine what it's like to outlive those you love?*

"Why keep doing it? Why stay alive?"

*Same as all of us. I seek my destiny. That purest expression of my essence. Heart Song, soul ballad, spiritual radiance – call it what you like.*

"Sounds like a lonely existence."

Light blue eyes staring at me. *We all make choices. You have to be clear about what you want. Every choice brings challenges. Every choice has a cost.*

"I understand."

*For me, an ordinary life was never enough. Hence, the extensive travels and numerous incarnations. Wealth, property, titles, adoration – those are illusory and unfulfilling. I now seek deeper penetration into the Mystery of Life.*

"How's that going for you?"

Silence descends upon us. Eventually he speaks. *Are you going to show me how this works?*

I demonstrate the time lines, the use of visualisation and intention to direct consciousness, and the importance of finding the glowing doors. "Uh, you cannot see them yet. Future You activated me somehow." I decide to keep Atra Atha a secret.

He stretches his arms expansively. *Such power … and responsibility … What's your game plan?*

"Ah. I am baffled at the moment. It has been a relentless chase, always two steps behind. I am more of a technology specialist than a strategist."

*Let's see … Apophis is trapped here on Earth. It's a wide net but a net nonetheless. He is not going anywhere.*

I nod.

*Your mistake has been the chase. He is very focused and goal-oriented. Discover what he covets and make him come to you.*

Slow blink. "That's brilliant."

Another smile. *You need to bait the trap. What do you know of this enemy?*

"Cunning, devious, highly intelligent, zero compassion. Won't hesitate to kill and destroy. Seeks an exit from this planet to fulfil his primary overarching mission."

Cronus casts a studious gaze. *And what is his primary mission?*

I suddenly realise the answer. "To annihilate you. Wipe out your existence."

The words surprise me. Have those thoughts been forming quietly in my unconscious?

The military strategist tilts his head aggressively. *Explain.*

"Sorry. It just dawned on me. Apophis is more than a practitioner of the dark arts. He is darkness. That's why he calls himself the Dark Lizard. He seeks to eradicate Life and obliterate the Light."

*To reduce Something to Nothing?*

"Exactly!"

*And how is that related to me?*

I raise my index finger sagely. "Apophis has probably been alive longer than you. Wait … his dark essence has always wrestled with Creation. Yes, that's it!"

Strange euphoria flowing through me … feel elated and kind of outside myself … Where is this information coming from?

Impatient snapping of fingers. *Tell me!*

"In the beginning there was Something and Nothing. By choosing to Love, the Something created and expanded, manifesting Itself as Light and Life. The Nothing, by its nature, could not create. It preferred to co-opt and corrupt Creation for nefarious purposes – ultimately to dissemble and annihilate it. As time went by, the Something became vastly more powerful than the Nothing, resulting in the Nothing becoming a constricted border around the Something.

"From time immemorial the Nothing had been defeated. As a last resort, the Nothing concocted a desperate and incisive strategy: Destroy Time. If Time was eradicated then everything that had been created would cease to exist. The Something would be obliterated or, at very least, unable to manifest. The Nothing would be free to reign supreme."

Cronus laughs heartily. *Apophis is an aspect of the Nothing. A piece of that Darkness.*

I grimace. "Even the label Darkness hints at something. It's just a word … a poor attempt to describe the Nothing. Nothing is in fact Nothing."

He raises his clenched fist and shouts *I will fulfil my destiny! I shall become a Time Lord! I will stand courageously against the Nothing!*

Wow. We are very different beings. I tend to be slightly apprehensive and cautious by nature … favouring deep and intimate relationships … Cronus appears to be a loner … a ragged courageous warrior … solitary … fiercely independent … passionate.

It's my turn to smile. "Your daughter is just like you."

*I can't wait to meet her.*

"Indeed."

My hand relaxes, drawing my attention. I notice that we are vice-gripping the same undulating time line. Shimmering with golden-white light, it seems woven into the fabric of the Time Stream. I try to follow the line but it's like staring into a blazing sun. My eyes hurt and I am forced to turn away. Whose time line is this?

Shaking my head … I grab Cronus' arm, visualise the time-place and exit. Bartholdi Park at sunset. I gaze at the rippling water for a while. That's quite enough for one day.

* * *

The new year has begun. Between the space project and advising JFK, we manage to slip away a few times a week to surf the Time Stream. Cronus says he feels at home for the first time in his long life. I have to smile. Only a recluse would call this undulating mass 'home'. The combination of our mental and spiritual aptitudes yields a lot more understanding of the Stream.

It is a few months before I am ready to show him Atra Atha. When I do, he is blown away. Initially nonplussed about my natural caution, Cronus gradually comes to appreciate the secrecy owed to such a powerful phenomenon. When I share the Time Lord's code – Power, Responsibility, Virtue – he nods respectfully.

It feels like a turning point in our relationship. Trust has been established and ideas are being exchanged. I sense a renewed vigour flowing through my spirit. Subtle changes are occurring within both of us. His military edginess is rubbing off on me, encouraging me to think more strategically. He has become focused and peaceful. I guess that's what happens when you meet your destiny.

July 1962 serves as a natural marker. That time-altering crash took place 15 years ago. The time-jumps make the event recent for me but it certainly slowed the Dark Lizard. Losing control of the master key must have been infuriating. Or perhaps it merely fuelled a dispassionate search for an escape from this planet.

Cronus and I are called to an urgent meeting with JFK. When we arrive at the Oval Office we notice his normal composure is absent. Jack looks kind of breathless and stern at the same time. Sitting on the edge of his desk, he leans forward anxiously. "I have just returned from Paradise Ranch. Where to begin?"

He stands up and paces across the room. "There are more Greys. Over one hundred of them. The CIA authorised and covertly funded an operation to create a specialised military force. In a couple of months an experimental spacecraft will take its first test flight."

Deep breath. Slowly exhale. How did they go from two to one hundred so quickly? Why was JFK kept in the dark?

He continues. "That is not the real issue. You warned me recently about meeting someone and getting the shivers. It has happened only once before. At the Ranch I was introduced to a senior lab technician, credited as the genius behind the cloning project. Apparently he usually shuns human interaction, preferring to work directly with the Greys, but he agreed to meet with me briefly. As soon as I moved into his presence … instant shivers … the blackest eyes … like looking into nothing … there was this strange moment ... as if he was entering my mind and he could see what I was thinking … caught a fleeting glimpse of his plan … then threatening energy … felt dizzy and a bit sick afterward."

Cronus and I glance at each other. "Apophis!"

JFK collapses into his cushioned rocking chair. "Something is wrong. Very, very wrong."

Those words are familiar. A sense of déjà vu grips my consciousness. Are we too late? Is this planet in danger? "Jack, what are we missing?"

Long silence. Staring out the window. Then he sits up, jaw tightening. "My hands are tied. This is strictly between us. Beyond top secret. You must assassinate Apophis."

Cronus responds immediately. *Consider it done.*

I voice my agreement. A blanket of solemn quietness settles upon us. Then we are promptly ushered out of the president's office.

Preparation is already complete. We've established the overarching mission of Apophis. As a dark being, an aspect of the Nothing, he wishes to destroy all Existence. Time is his primary target, introducing a battle which Cronus is clearly relishing.

I am no longer feeling that undercurrent of confusion and fear. We have a plan to draw out the Dark Lizard. What he seeks most is advanced technology to facilitate his escape from primitive Earth. And we will provide it. Cronus intends to surreptitiously spread a rumour about the development of a Light weapon at Wright-Patterson Air Force Base. Yep, we are using the Vajra as bait.

Sitting at the military weapons-testing range, I try to recall the instructions. The only words were 'touch to activate'. Removing the Vajra from my necklace ... press ... suddenly it expands to the size of a barbell ... brilliant and semi-translucent ... comprising a bar, which seems to form a natural grip, with a spindle on each end ... the spokes of the spindle can be twisted open ... my wrist twitches and the weapon fires a light beam with an unexpected scchhh! I drop it in shock and Cronus bursts out laughing.

*Give it here.*

Reluctantly I hand it over.

He makes it look so simple. The weapon can be fired in both directions if the spindles on each end are open. Twist open the spokes then squeeze the bar. Scchhh! To shrink the weapon back to necklace size, close both spindles then squeeze the bar. Amazing.

Life on the base becomes a comfortable routine. Attending lectures in the morning – military strategy, leadership, command, ethics, innovation, survival. Practical training exercises in the afternoon. Mastering the Vajra at every opportunity. After a few weeks I look down at my belly and smile. Ha, Maya, it's not so soft anymore!

Cronus and I keep ourselves busy, often taking long walks in the nearby parks. We don't mind the waiting game. It is likely that word has already reached Apophis; however, his attention is probably on the impending test flight.

One afternoon two servicemen approach as we are strolling along the deserted far end of the base. It's a casual friendly conversation about life in the military. All smiles and mild banter. After a while I detect a slight shift in the energy field. The tone of voice becomes a little edgy. One of the men enquires about Cronus' role in weapons development. You know that moment – you can feel it – something is about to happen. It's that weird space where everyone is aware of an imminent action but on the surface things seem calm and composed. The movements you make at this point are critical to a successful outcome.

I cough softly and remove the Vajra from my necklace. It lies secretly in the palm of my hand. Cronus notices the covert motion and immediately stretches and turns away from me. He walks a couple of steps and begins to discuss the new weapon, creating a suitable distraction. I activate the Vajra behind my back, turning one of the spindles. Suddenly a firearm is pointing at Cronus. The blue-white beam fires with a scchhh! and the serviceman falls. Immediately he shifts to his natural state, revealing his true identity. It's a Grey.

I train the Vajra on the remaining being. No need for deception anymore. For a few seconds nobody moves, then the energy field flickers and fades. The Grey looks at me closely. I quickly shield my mind and shout "Did Apophis send you?" The loudness of my voice surprises me.

He nods slowly. My nerves are all over the place. Cronus calmly takes over, relieving me of the Vajra. *What are your intentions?*

Stoical expression. "Create an army. Destroy your world. Follow Apophis."

Big smile. *Not if we destroy you first.*

"MJ-12 will never allow that."

*MJ-who?*

The Grey levels a weapon, leaving Cronus little choice. A deft squeeze. Scchhh! Brief pause. Then he vaporises both bodies with repeated blasts of light.

*No evidence. Less complications.*

Shaken, I get to my feet and retrieve the Vajra. Safely stow it on my necklace. "This is not the end, is it?"

Cronus gazes at me earnestly. *More will come. Apophis uses the Greys to do his dirty work.*

"We need to warn JFK."

*That we do.*

We hurry over to the base commander's office to make a phone call. It takes me about half an hour to relax into my normal state. The world I come from is saturated in peace and harmony. Harsh conflict is foreign and frightening to me. Sadly we have to take defensive action to protect and preserve this planet.

I sit on a wooden chair while Cronus arranges a meeting with Jack. Apophis clearly has a strategy and is gaining the upper hand once more. I stare at the ground. Hang on … in all the tumult … almost forgot … what on earth is MJ-12?

* * *

It's November. The leaves tumble and dance across the ground. We are warmly ensconced in JFK's office. Cronus is describing the recent altercation and confirming the president's worst fears.

I interject. "Obviously I know about Apophis' mission. And Cronus learned because of his destiny. My question is: How did you discover his plan? Was it accidental? Were you deliberately allowed a glimpse? Is it an arrogant taunt?"

Jack shakes his head. "You said he can invade consciousness. I felt him in my mind. He must have seen you, Indra. Perhaps he was firing a warning shot to scare us away. Whatever the reason, we are now in a precarious position. Unfortunately only three people on the planet know his true agenda."

A disconcerting quietness envelops the room.

Eventually I ask "Have you told us everything? The Grey hinted that MJ-12 is in charge. What does that mean?"

Deep sigh. Fingers massaging his temples. "You better sit down. What I am going to tell you is above top secret."

Cronus and I move away from the tall windows and recline on the off-white sofa.

"1947 was a precipitous year for our country. The Roswell crash occurred on 7 July, introducing an unprecedented threat to national security. Our reaction was swift and rigorous. The U.S. Army Air Corps officially became the U.S. Air Force on 26 July. The CIA was founded on 18 September. Majestic-12 was established on 24 September.

"Majestic-12 is a consortium of very powerful people. It comprises six high-ranking government, military and intelligence officials; three civilian scientists, specialising in physics, aeronautical engineering and aviation; and three chiefs of industry and commerce. All sworn to total secrecy. MJ-12 is charged with exploiting alien technology to benefit and defend the United States of America. It reports directly to the incumbent president."

Why should I be surprised? It seems we all have our secrets.

"MJ-12 oversees the monitoring, harvesting, cloning and reverse-engineering of alien life forms and technology; appropriates advanced data and information systems; gathers intelligence to strengthen national security; and spreads disinformation to prevent public or foreign disclosure of the alien presence."

A murmur from Cronus. *That's a whole lot of Power and Responsibility. Where's the Virtue?*

Jack frowns. "We have gained so much from our interaction with the Greys. Consequently, my recent warnings to the group have been derided. No one wants to believe that we are not in control. No one is willing to consider that we might be serving an alien agenda. I am becoming a lone voice in the wilderness. And powerful vested interests are moving the group beyond my command. Hence, my original request: Take out Apophis. It's the only way to prevent a global cataclysm."

A fervent discussion ensues. President Kennedy cannot be implicated nor bear any association with our offensive or defensive activities. There will be no government or military support if our 'treachery' is discovered. We surmise that Apophis is aware of my existence so Cronus will remain the primary link between me and JFK. In terms of strategy, a direct assault or invasion at Paradise Ranch is untenable – we would be outmanned, outgunned and risk extensive collateral damage. We have no choice but to continue our bait-and-trap operation.

When we finally leave the president's office, I offer a warm handshake. "Take care of yourself, Jack."

Things heat up considerably over the next few months. The first successful test flight of a human-alien spacecraft takes place in late January 1963. Under Apophis' supervision the Greys, now numbering 140, work all hours to perfect aeronautic and weapon systems.

February through May we experience minor skirmishes with Greys in remote locations. Although we always erase evidence of our battles and cloud the minds of any witnesses, we are chagrined to discover newspapers reporting a new phenomenon, termed 'Men in Black'. This attracts undue attention and makes our operation more difficult. Things escalate significantly in July when we are attacked by a spacecraft from Area 51 and successfully blast the ship out of the sky. News stories begin connecting UFOs and Men in Black, forcing Majestic-12 to step up its disinformation campaign.

Word reaches us in August that a fleet of 30 spaceships is on the verge of completion. JFK has become adamant about the dangers facing the planet, which naturally alienates him from the ultra-secret group. As for us, the July battle exposed our existence and we are no longer able to hide in plain sight. It is just a matter of time before we become enemies of the state.

We are on the run. Being hunted. I am grateful for the vast military experience of Cronus. A couple of brilliant ambushes destroy three more spacecraft and reduce the Grey headcount by a further seven. My competence and confidence increase every day.

In October we get a call from JFK, asking us to meet him at Edwards Air Force Base which is located in the Mojave Desert northeast of Los Angeles. When we arrive a Colonel escorts us to the bombing range. Jack is waving in the distance. I can vaguely make out his welcoming smile. "Come on over," he shouts, "I want to show you something."

Exiting the vehicle, adopting a brisk pace. Strange sensation prickling my awareness. Tiny specks appearing over the nearby mountain range. The movement is familiar … objects rapidly increasing in size … Greys! Breaking into a run, arms flailing. "Jack! Jack! You need to take cover!" Still smiling. Unmoving. Confused. Everything seems to slow. Cronus rushes ahead … it's not right … I've got the shivers … releasing the Vajra, turning both spindles … "Cronus, stop!" … moving in front of me, obscuring JFK … my legs feel heavy … drop to one knee … weapon at shoulder height … wait for it … wait … two ships flank me … squeeze the bar … shocks of light … thunderous destruction …

A shot rings out … I turn my head … Cronus is on the ground … JFK crouching over him, searching his pockets … close one spindle … line up another ship … squeeze … run toward them … Jack has the master key in his hand … what on earth? … a terrible whump nearby … too many ships … firing the Vajra … dark blue light above the president … beamed aboard a spacecraft … firing and firing … suddenly a mass exodus …

Alone. The sky is empty. Dark smoke swirling across the ground. "Cronus!" Roll him over. Blood everywhere. "What happened?"

Faint whisper. *Apophis.*

Not again! This can't be happening. Is Cronus destined to die repeatedly at the hands of the Dark Lizard? Is there nothing I can do to prevent this pattern?

Grips my shoulder. *Cloud the mind of the Colonel … bring him closer … transfer my consciousness …*

I act quickly. A few minutes later his body expires and soft light streaks across the Colonel's face. "Cronus? Is that you?"

*Indra … remain still … repressing consciousness … hmm, interesting experiences … yep, that will do.*

"Really? What happens to the Colonel's mind?"

*It's only temporary. I obviously prefer a newly created body. His voice is suddenly urgent. Pay attention: That wasn't Jack. Apophis has regained control of the master key. You don't belong here. I do. Give me the Vajra. Leap into the Time Stream. They will think we are both deceased. It's the only way.*

"But what about you?"

*Jump ahead. Keep an eye on Apophis. Memorise my face. Meet me 15 November 1963 at Bartholdi Park. Go!*

The plan makes sense. I hurriedly look for a glowing portal and make the leap. Flow to Atra Atha, enter the Immersion and find the relevant time lines. Move forward two weeks. Area 51. Greys now totalling 122. Frenetic activity. A large cigar-shaped spacecraft designated as the 'Battleship' is being retrofitted to function with the master key. They must have cracked the Time Key's code. Final checks on the remaining saucer-shaped craft. Apophis intends to make his escape!

This planet may be in grave danger. Return to the Stream. Visualise the date. Exit through the Conservatory door. A couple of hours later the Colonel appears. I stand calmly near the fountain, taking care to keep my body language subdued. A big smile. *Indra!* Phew, it's him.

"Hey, how's the body?"

*Fit and healthy. Want to hear the good news? The Colonel has clearance for Paradise Ranch.*

Synchronicity. I tell him about the latest developments.

Cronus rubs his chin thoughtfully. *You're not going to like this. Find a way to warn JFK. And do not interfere with my impending actions. Just observe the events. You may have to pick up the pieces afterward.*

I swallow hard. "Why? Where are you going?"

He laughs tempestuously. *Area 51, of course. So much is at stake. It's time for a showdown.* Solemn pause. *It's been great working with you. You have shown me so much.*

A hug feels inappropriate. I bow respectfully, turn on my heel and enter the Stream. Into the Immersion. Scanning … Aha! The White House Rose Garden leads to the east door of the Oval Office, and that entrance is covered in undulating blue waves. Perfect access point. Moving along the time line … there, he is alone … time-place Monday, 18 November 1963.

Tentatively open the door. He is in his rocking chair, perusing a document. I cough softly but still manage to startle him. The famous smile beams toward me. "Indra! Come in, sit down on the sofa. How are you?"

I glance at the document. It's an itinerary. "You going somewhere, Jack?"

"Texas. On Thursday and Friday. I must finalise the motorcade route so we can release it to the public by end of day."

A momentary shiver. "We need to talk."

The northwest door of the Oval Office bursts open and in strides a determined gentleman. "Hello, Jack." He immediately extends his hand. "Bobby Kennedy. Don't think we've met."

"Indra Black, Technology Consultant."

"Sit down, both of you. This is my brother Robert Francis Kennedy, also known as RFK. Best friend, confidant and political adviser. Serving as Attorney General of this fine country. Anything you want to say can be shared openly."

Oh. What happened to 'beyond top secret' and 'only three people on the planet'? Anyway, it's none of my business. They're in charge. I catch them up with recent events.

Bobby and Jack look knowingly at each other. Finally JFK speaks. "A week ago I ordered MJ-12 to publicly disclose the entire Majestic Operation. I believe it is in the best interests of America and the world. Advanced technology should be used to eradicate poverty, disease and war. I also instructed them to immediately shut down the militarisation project."

Wow. I did not see that coming. "How did they take it?"

"Mixed reactions. The members are very powerful, influential and wealthy, with connections to the highest echelons of military, government and industry. I am convinced they will accede to my request. They have until 30 November."

I raise my hands. "Things seem to be reaching a critical point."

"It's going to be alright, Indra. Now, I have a busy week ahead. Do you mind if I have a chat with Bobby?"

A courteous bow. "Best of luck to both of you."

I leave through the east door. It feels kind of lonely. Nothing to do but watch events unfold from the Time Stream.

Back in Atra Atha. Enter the Immersion. Grab a time line in each hand, settle into the shimmering mist. I sigh deeply. This place seriously needs a reclining leather armchair.

AREA 51: Cronus arrives in the late morning on Friday 22 November 1963. Security appears rather relaxed; perhaps the base is winding down for the weekend. A soundless movement draws his gaze: Departure of the Battleship and 11 saucer-shaped spacecraft; destination unknown. He proceeds to the Research and Development Centre within the Black Hangar. Havoc and mayhem ensue. Deft use of the Vajra obliterates 95 of the remaining 109 Greys and 5 of the remaining 9 spaceships. Overwhelmed by gunfire. Slumps to the ground with a strange smile on his face. At the last possible moment, transfers his consciousness to the nearest available being. Laughter grips me. Cronus is now inside a Grey! I watch him wrestle quietly for a few minutes then mingle indifferently with the rest of the crew. An impressive performance.

My brow furrows. What am I missing? Scanning the time line ... Apophis is on the Battleship ... accompanied by 11 Greys on 11 ships ... shaking my head ... what is it? ... oh ... the math does not add up ... there should have been 111 Greys and 10 ships remaining in the hangar. Where is the absent spacecraft and two Greys?

I move back a few hours and watch the launch of a single ship. Two humans carrying high-powered rifles climb on board, accompanied by two Greys. Tracking its movements. Dallas, Texas. Wait a minute. Jack's itinerary. His time line is still in my other hand.

JFK: Thursday 21 November 1963. Time-place ... Texas ... San Antonio – dedication speech for U.S. Air Force School of Aerospace Medicine ... Houston – testimonial dinner at the Rice Hotel ... Fort Worth – overnight at Texas Hotel ... Friday 22 November ... Chamber of Commerce breakfast speech at same hotel ... Jack, Jacqueline and presidential entourage boarding Air Force One ... short flight to Dallas ... arrive in Love Field ... motorcade begins journey to Trade Mart ... the two time lines are twisting together ... uneasy feeling ... motorcade entering Dealey Plaza ... multiple gunshots resounding! ... panicky sensation ... shock ... horror ... racing to nearby hospital ... frantic attempt to save the president ... pronounced dead at 1.00 pm ... stunned ... JFK has been assassinated.

Unable to move. Bewildered. Can't believe what I have just witnessed. Who would dare assassinate a president? What am I doing wrong? Why can't I prevent this relentless mayhem and devastation? My world is gone. And something dark has descended on this planet. Apophis. That purveyor of destruction.

At least I am alive. I must not give up the mission. Cronus is safe. Wait. Bobby Kennedy! He knows too much. Grab his time line ... grief ... anger ... threats ... move forward ... refusal to cooperate or stay silent ... wins the California Democratic primary on 5 June 1968 ... set to challenge Richard Nixon for the White House

… finishes victory speech at the Ambassador hotel in Los Angeles … shaking hands with kitchen staff … multiple gunshots! ... inconceivable … both Kennedys have been assassinated!

Should I jump back and warn RFK? Is there a way I can stop this murder? I grab Apophis' time line. Dread fills me. So distressed by these events … forgot the threat … the Grey at Wright-Patterson Air Force Base spoke of plans to destroy this planet … surf back to Area 51 … exodus of the Battleship and 11 spacecraft … tracking their flight across the United States … positioning over military bases … superior weaponry … it's too late … strange … Cronus' line is intersecting … a Grey reports the obliteration at the Black Hangar … warns Apophis of a formidable Light weapon that is invisible and indestructible.

I sense the Dark Lizard wavering … weighing the risks … the ambience feels dense … heavy … my body is shaking with trepidation … then he turns away … gathers his forces … unexpectedly launches every ship through a glowing portal and into the Time Stream … flood of relief … Earth has been spared.

I watch his army travelling back in time … same old strategy … if at first you don't succeed, go to an earlier period and try, try again … it forces me to continually play catch-up … what is his destination? … oh no … a few thousand years into the past … but still planet Earth …

Why Earth? Has he got a score to settle? I cannot afford to hang around. Must keep my focus on the overall mission. Earth is safe in this time period but my planet still needs rescuing. Apophis and his entourage must be stopped. I take a deep breath, leap into the Stream and follow the quivering dark line.

* * *

I hate doing this ... flying blind after the Dark Lizard. Never knowing what to expect. My comfortable life on Mani seems so far away. I miss Priya. We had such great dreams ... hopes ... a sweet memory flits across my mind ... holding hands and walking along a tree-lined avenue in the glorious sunshine ... have to accept that she is gone ... as painful as it is ... she was terminated after delivering the apprentice's key ... and the planets orbiting Arcturus were destroyed.

The glowing door pulses toward me. Need to think like Cronus. Be a strategist. My beloved world needs aggressive protection. Peace and security come at a price. It's not all rainbows and butterflies anymore. These are hard realities and I feel painfully aware of my responsibilities. Wow. What has happened to me?

I walk out into the blazing sun of Egypt. The Immersion calls this site Lunu which means Place of Pillars. It is also known as City of the Sun. My image projector helps me blend in with the local populace: Deeply tanned skin ... wrap-around white linen skirt, known as a shendyt, belted at the waist ... jewellery is popular so I manifest a gorgerine, an assembly of metal discs worn on the chest ... and papyrus sandals, usually reserved for priests. I look neither like a labourer nor a pharaoh. No one should bother me.

Tracking down Apophis and the Greys will be no easy task. Unlike me, who can only project an illusory image, they can actually shape-shift. Hmm ... that makes no sense ... Apophis is a different kind of being ... I speculate half physical, half energetic ... he can definitely shape-shift ... but the Greys are physical clones ... they must be using similar technology to me. I shall have to uncover the switching apparatus. As for their ships, they are obviously invisible and already well hidden.

Trying to get my bearings in this strange land. The Nile is the longest river on the planet – the Amazon is a close second – flowing approximately 6,680 kilometres (4,150 miles in ancient measurement) from East Africa northward to the Mediterranean. Predictable annual flooding deposits rich soil across the fertile valley, creating ideal agricultural conditions. Recurrent surplus crops have allowed the nation to explore and develop diverse aspects of society and culture.

Lunu (according to the Immersion later renamed Heliopolis) is located at the beginning of the Nile Delta in Lower Egypt (Northern Egypt). This is where the river divides and spreads over a vast region before draining into the sea.

Sitting on the stone steps of a temple, wondering how to proceed. Connections are important; having allies in the battle against Apophis has proven valuable. I look down at the peculiar animal winding itself affectionately around my legs. Sacred to the Egyptians, cats are probably revered because of their ability to catch rats, mice and snakes. Statues of felines are placed outside numerous buildings.

Sleek and muscular … scarab beetle marking on its forehead … long dark stripe running along the spine from head to tail … intense green eyes gazing up at me …

*You're not from around here, are you?*

Startled, I stare nervously at the bronze short-haired cat.

*Relax. Your form is visible to me. I will not harm you.*

"As far as I know, cats cannot speak."

The eyes twinkle. *Perhaps I am not really a cat.*

"Who are you?"

*Baset, the protector and defender of Ra. Also known as the Lady of Flame and Eye of Ra.*

"Ra?"

*The god of light. Ra means 'sun' or 'creative power'. So named because he originates from the sun.*

"Wait a minute. Which sun?"

She looks up. *That one.*

"I have heard of Ra. In my time he is located in the star Arcturus."

*Arcturus?*

"Yeah. It's an enormous star about 180 times more luminous than your sun."

*What did you mean by 'in my time'?*

Oops.

"Uh, can we just skip that part?"

*I think Ra would really like to meet you.*

"I would really like to meet Ra."

She turns her head, beckoning me to follow. We pad along the streets until we reach a colossal temple. Up the shimmering steps and into a huge courtyard sprinkled with imposing statues and towering obelisks. Ushered into an immense hall … marble pillars standing like sentries guarding each side … above me bright sky refracting through a crystal dome … truly spectacular …

Glowing bald-headed man in a white robe approaching. I swallow apprehensively. Swift slap to my shoulder. *You can drop that image now. Show me your true form.*

I touch the bracelet and bow respectfully.

It takes a few minutes to adjust to the penetrating stare of his luminous blue eyes. After a while he nods solemnly. *Don't know your species. Where are you from?*

Here we go again. Breaching the time law. I am probably going to pay for this one day.

"Arcturus of the Boötes constellation, approximately thirty-six light years from Earth. My beautiful planet was attacked by an unseen enemy and subsequently obliterated. As far as I know, there are only two of us left. Arcturians were the leaders of this galaxy. Keeping peace between the various planets, advancing the ideals of love and harmony. Our genetic code was perfected in the last millennium. This is our current form."

*Experience has taught me that each being must prove its virtue. Words are empty. Actions count.*

Wow. He's a bit brusque.

*You never mentioned your name.*

"Indra, at your service."

*Why are you here, Indra?*

"I am chasing a formidable dark being. He is the catalyst that destroyed my world. Cunning, devious and dispassionate. Every time I get close, he jumps further back in time, creating numerous ripples and disruptions in the Time Stream."

*You travel through time.*

"I do."

*How interesting. Dangerous, egocentric and irresponsible.*

"Indeed. That is why it was banned throughout the galaxy. Only the Time Lord may surf the Stream."

*Are you a renegade?*

"The Time Lord deputised me just before his death. The enemy shows no discrimination and intends to destroy all worlds. My mission is to prevent the annihilation of All That Is."

A flicker of a smile. *That burden must weigh heavily on you.*

"You have no idea."

*The being we met yesterday told us a similar story. Apep portrays himself as an innocent star traveller, visiting worlds to exchange knowledge and technology. Most of his compatriots were recently destroyed by an unseen enemy. He made his escape but believes he is being stalked by a vicious protagonist. He also claims to be able to travel through time.*

Rendered speechless. This is not what I expected.

*Which of you speaks the truth?*

There is nothing to say.

*I advise you to tread carefully. The gods of light intend to progress the spiritual and technological development of the human race. Interference would be perilous.*

Ironic.

*My beautiful Egyptian Mau will be keeping an eye on both of you.*

I nod deferentially.

*Go now.*

The sleek cat escorts me back to the street. A cute miaow, then *Don't worry about him. Bark is worse than his bite. As long as you are truthful, you'll be alright.*

Is that an ominous or friendly warning?

"Listen, Apep has an army. Don't trust anything he says or does."

Her tail wraps around my ankle. *We've been around for a while. Nothing we can't handle.*

I retrieve my leg and sigh deeply. A curt wave and frustrated departure. Strolling through the streets aimlessly … ah, palm trees … trickling water … collapse beneath the expansive fronds and close my eyes … cool breeze … tired of feeling helpless and out of control … a bystander amid constant chaos and destruction …

"Hey, stranger."

Vague outline. Focus my gaze. Local female, wearing a beaded sheath dress known as a kalasiri, adorned with dazzling turquoise and silver jewellery.

"Do I know you?"

"Hope so. Otherwise I've come a long way for nothing."

Perplexed silence. "Maya?"

Slow nod.

"How do I know it's you?"

"Push the mauve stone on your bracelet. It temporarily disrupts incoming waves."

"Oh. It is you. Why didn't you teach me that before?"

Shrug. "Didn't think you would need it. You do now."

"Where have you been?"

She sits alongside me and places her hand gently into the water. "Had my own skirmishes with Apophis. Scoured vast areas after the crash. Observed you retrieving the Time Key. Realised that he was trapped on Earth. Consequently ran a series of mini time loops, trying to arrive just before him at various time-places."

"How did that work out?"

"You were following your own strategy. The long game. And it worked. You and Cronus saved Earth. I focused on chasing down Apophis in order to retrieve the time-dilation ring. Figured that would severely impede his plans, especially after having lost the Time Key. Despite his immense intelligence, he has a weakness: Arrogance. Completely underestimates his opponents. That trait cost him four fingers."

She extends her hand and flashes the ring.

"Wow, Maya. Well done!" I scrutinise the shiny black stone encompassed by fine silver. "Is that obsidian?"

"Yep. Sparkling and intense."

I smile. "A bit like you."

She glances at me sternly. "Had your back on more than one occasion."

"You did?"

"You're alive, aren't you?"

"Indeed I am. Truly grateful."

It is good to have company. Her words have lifted my spirit. Perhaps I am not completely useless after all.

The great thing about being an Arcturian is that we do not need to eat or drink. Also, our portable energy shields automatically provide personal protection. It is not long before we are both asleep, lulled by the soporific sounds of the bubbling water.

***

I wake to find her head in my lap. This should be interesting. Half an hour later she rouses, registers her position and pulls back immediately. Knew it. Too much intimacy for a fiercely independent lone ranger.

It is a beautiful new day. Dawn rays are peeking across the horizon. The fluttering of ibis and waterfowl in the river is counterpointed by the darting of a falcon high overhead. A few metres to one side an old man unloads a small cart and prepares to decorate his reddish-brown pottery. Unmoving, I stare at the rising sun. Eventually a yawn and long stretch overtake me.

A furry tail brushes just beneath my nose. "Morning, Baset. Come to harass me already?"

*I thought you might introduce me to your friend.*

"Baset, Maya."

"Oh. It talks."

"Yes it does. And she works for Ra."

"The sun-god?"

"The very same."

Although Arcturians do not have a physical gender, our traits tend to vaguely define us as masculine or feminine. It is a rather pointless carry-over from a previous chapter in our very long history. So I guess it's alright to say that the two females quickly establish a close connection. The animated conversation between Baset and Maya prompts me to go for a walk. I generally prefer quietude.

Meandering along the streets. Maybe the women will come up with a plan because I have no idea what to do. Even if I met Apophis, and on the off-chance could outmanoeuvre him, I would still have to contend with Ra. He will be watching us like a hawk. No one wants to incur his wrath.

If I have learned anything about strategy, it is this: There are times when it is better to wait for your opponent to make the wrong move. Blindly rushing in may have dire consequences. The Dark Lizard is surely aware that Maya and I have followed him to this time-place. But his actions will be as restricted as ours. Perhaps I have judged myself too harshly. There is value in playing the long game.

Later in the day Maya joins my exploratory ambling. "Baset has agreed not to reveal our identities to Apophis. She promises that Ra will honour that commitment too. It will give us more scope to operate and lessen the tension. We better get used to life in ancient Egypt."

"Would you like to cuddle?" I gesture playfully.

"No!"

"Surprised to see you two getting along so well. Thought you prefer your own company."

"Interesting cat. Erudite, eloquent, strong and graceful."

"You want to be her when you grow up?"

"Ha ha." Is that a grimace or pout?

"So what's the strategy?"

She places her hands on hips. "If it was up to me, I'd go in with guns blazing. But we need to proceed with caution." Brief pause. "We have the time-dilation ring. That must give us some advantage."

"Yeah, for the wearer."

"Not true. If we hold hands both of us are ensconced in the time-dilation field."

"You want to hold hands with me?"

"If I must ..."

I am about to burst into laughter. This is going to be fun. Suddenly a tall figure with an elongated head rounds the corner. Dressed in a long white robe with leopard skin draped across his shoulders. Surrounded by an entourage. Instantly I get the shivers. Maya slips her hand into mine and holds tightly.

When they finally pass, I sigh with relief. "Thanks for protecting us."

"Uh, I wasn't. Too little time to activate the ring. Besides, he won't scan our energy unless he suspects something."

"I was staring right at him."

"Yeah, I noticed."

"Wait a minute. Why were you holding my hand?"

"Was I?" She averts her gaze.

"You were scared too?"

Shrugs. "Maybe a little."

Huh. She sure hides her vulnerability well. I touch her gently on the shoulder. "Come on. Let's continue our walk."

"Follow him?"

"Yeah. From a safe distance. If anything happens grab my hand and turn the ring."

"What's the plan?"

"Observe him and exploit his weaknesses. We may even discover the location of his ships."

We quicken our pace until the royal group comes into view. After a few minutes I push the mauve stone on my bracelet. The misty apparitions disperse. Greys! I count nine of them which means two have probably remained with the ships. I feel Maya slipping her hand into mine again.

I cannot see Apophis. Where is he? Terrible sensation. Behind us. *You insignificant fleas! Did you think I would not see you immediately?*

Maya dials the ring. Everything outside the field slows.

*I know who you are, Indra and Maya of Mani. The planets orbiting Arcturus are gone. You have no home.*

Touching my necklace. Oh. Cronus still has the Vajra.

*You cannot hide from me. After I destroy those you love, I will come for you. Death is inevitable.*

He hails his entourage and leads them away from us. After a few minutes Maya dials back the ring. Her body is quivering. "That plan did not go well."

I put my arm around her shoulders. “True. At least we know we are not invisible. We will have to be more careful. And we understand his primary objective.”

“We do?”

“He intends to destroy the earliest incarnation of your father.”

She is quiet for a few moments. “For what purpose?”

“To become the Time Lord. Then obliterate Time.”

“Is that possible?”

“Perhaps the Time Stream can be erased.”

“That’s abhorrent. It would effectively destroy Life.”

“And Light.”

“Indra, we have to stop him.”

“We will.” My brow furrows. “I think it’s time to visit Atra Atha.”

Maya locates the nearest portal and we make the jump. Hopefully Apophis is still busy on the ground. We don’t want to run into him here.

***

The time line of Cronus is full of extraordinary twists and turns. It appears the shrewd Time Lord has deliberately attempted to obscure his origins. Endless loops upon loops discourage even the most determined investigator.

We monitor Apophis from the Stream and on the planet. He is posing as a benevolent guardian of the human race and has agreed to combine forces with Ra to assist Earth. Does he still sting from the beating he took at Area 51? Or is he heedful of the sun-god's reputation and power? Either way, we have no choice but to watch in awe as Ra and the Dark Lizard spend the next few years working in harmony to develop humankind. Together they spread advanced teachings on architecture, construction, agriculture, mathematics and writing. As the trust matures, Ra begins to share his knowledge and technology with Apophis.

And I thought we were playing the long game.

Even though we have located his ships, and experienced numerous opportunities to obliterate individual Greys, we cannot afford to strike. The Dark Lizard's smoke-and-mirrors strategy has swayed the minds of the Egyptian people, making him as popular and respected as Ra. Attacking his entourage would frame us as aggressors. We can do nothing except watch and wait.

Arcturians need only 3-4 hours rest in every 24 hour cycle. That leaves us with much free time. Maya regularly disappears with Baset to learn various forms of dance. On occasion she demonstrates her beautiful natural rhythm in disparate harem, festival and combat dances. As the months go by, she also takes up diverse musical instruments, gradually favouring the harp. Her constant progress and increasing prowess are admirable.

I prefer my solitude. Her busy schedule affords me plenty of opportunity to gaze at the shimmering water and meditate under the protective palm fronds. Although we sometimes sleep in the Time Stream or on board Maya's spacecraft, most of the time we drift off by the gurgling river. Almost every morning the same old man unloads his pottery a few metres from us and begins painting.

One day I walk over and strike up a conversation. Introducing himself simply as the Artisan, he shows me his work. The pots and urns are magnificent. Later we meander down the streets until we reach a studio recessed in a dark alley. Larger than it appears from outside, the workshop displays an array of stone statues, fine reliefs, sumptuous pottery and resplendent paintings. There is something about his energy that I find intriguing. When he offers me an apprenticeship two weeks later, I readily accept.

And so begins my tranquil journey into the world of art. I learn to gather the Nile clay and mix it with straw and sand. Knead, coil and pinch. The hand-operated wheel is laborious but easier to rotate with two people. The first items to survive firing in the kiln are not pretty. Thankfully the Artisan has a sense of humour. It takes months of practice to master the techniques. Sometimes we acquire marl clay from the Qena region in Upper Egypt which results in a more refined and superior product. We burnish these pieces to a lustrous finish then fire them, leaving a blank canvas for decorating. Paints are derived from iron ores (red and yellow ochre), copper ores (blue and green), charcoal (black) and limestone (white). We carefully apply popular cultural patterns and symbols, including depictions of humans, animals, birds and boats. Successful completion of each piece brings me resounding joy.

At the end of each day Maya and I gaze at the brilliant sunset and trade entertaining stories. It's a bizarre situation. Both of us trying to save our planet and the people we love, yet spending our time apprenticing to the arts. I was married but lost my wife; now I fall asleep every night next to another female. For someone disposed to deep intimate relationships, the situation is very challenging.

On top of that, I have gradually hardened into a pragmatic strategist and Maya is clearly a quick-tempered passionate warrior like her father, but we are constrained by circumstances beyond our control. Every loitering month heightens the niggle that my soft belly is returning and that I won't be ready for the inevitable battle.

The loneliness is getting to me too. Solitude (enjoying one's own company) and loneliness (not feeling connected to one's family, friends, culture, nation or planet) are very different things. Since the demise of Mani and being hurled into the Time Stream I have only managed brief and fleeting interactions with other beings. I am completely displaced and emotionally empty.

One afternoon I am struggling to finish a bowl on the potter's wheel. No matter what I do it won't form the required precise shape. Exasperated, I shout my frustration across the room. The Artisan strolls over and scrutinises my slumped clay. He sits down and looks at me kindly. "You are not moving with the Flow. Your pain results from seeing yourself as separate to the clay. You are both the Creator and the Creation. Stop trying to force things to be different and work with what is trying to manifest. Close your eyes and learn to feel the energy."

Such obscure and mystical remarks were common on Mani. Every Arcturian planet was protected by a Cosmic Energy Shield, allowing us to live in unfettered peace and harmony. Beings walked upon their worlds with impeccability, integrity, compassion and loving-kindness. Everyone worked to serve their communities, societies and countries. Our abundant leisure time was reserved for pleasure and personal pursuits.

I never had to face constant chafing, challenges and obstacles. Loss, isolation, violence, defence, military strategy – those were concepts foreign to me.

The Artisan interrupts my thoughts. "Here are two Wills: Creation and Creator. Flow occurs when these Wills align. The clay needs to surrender to the potter's lofty perspective and sage experience. The potter needs to honour the song within the clay. An intimate conversation is required."

Sighing. Knead it back into a mound. Place my hands over it. Close my eyes. Who are you? What are you? What are you destined to become? My hands begin moving. I sense the presence of the clay ... its inner light ... pressing, kneading, coiling ... turning the wheel ... it's tall ... curvaceous ... pinch a spout ... shape a handle ... flowing ... turning ... wetting ... I open my eyes ...

perfect water jug … graceful … elegant … the manifestation of an innate song … a graceful heartbeat …

"Thank you." I bow gratefully to the Artisan.

Later in the evening I am chatting with Maya in the Time Stream. Have a strange sense of relief and a renewed freedom.

"Did you have a good day?"

She smiles happily. "The usual. Ambling around with Baset. Harp lesson. Absorbing the magnificent natural world of this planet."

"Natural world?"

"Animals, plants, trees, flowers, rivers. Appreciating the marvellous interaction of climate, landscape and living things."

"Are you falling in love with Earth?"

"A little. Baset and I have flown over many beautiful countries."

"You have?"

She nods. "Being stuck here has made me wonder if there is some grand plan. What if it is not just our will in operation? What if there is a greater force orchestrating events? What if we are part of something truly wondrous?"

"What do you mean?"

"Consider this: We are doing the best we can. Maybe our will is the direct result of our inner blueprint. Like a particular flower that is naturally destined to manifest with a certain shape, colour and scent. How much choice does it have?"

"Expand that thought for me."

"Every independent point of consciousness is instinctively trying to manifest its –"

"Heart Song?"

"Exactly! And get its needs met."

"Needs?"

"Spiritual, psychological, emotional, physical, energetic."

"Aha." I understand. "Each flower is trying to manifest its essence and obtain sufficient sun, rain and nutrients."

"Yes! And around each flower is a subtle swirling invisible force … an ephemeral hint … a whisper from the universe …"

"The divine aether?"

"Are you reading my mind, Indra?" She giggles playfully.

"Uh, no … everything you are saying makes sense … but how is that related to us?"

"We have been struggling against that formidable Dark Lizard for so long … we need to surrender and align with the divine aether …" Her eyes look almost hypnotic. "Surrender and flow, surrender and flow."

"Do less?"

"No … keep doing the best we can … manifesting our essence … trying to satisfy our needs … save our world … also surrender and flow … surrender and flow …"

Her words are making me feel strange and disoriented … slightly euphoric …

"My dear Indra. There is nothing to fear. Who said that Darkness can extinguish the Light? We are witnesses to the Universe in motion. The journey of All That Is. Nothing cannot create Something. Something has always existed. Nothing exists alongside Something. Nothing cannot destroy Something. It is the nature of Something to create Something. Something will always exist."

Abstruse and esoteric teaching … everything swirling … bright white light … elated …

Déjà vu. We are vice-gripping the same undulating time line. Shimmering with golden-white light, it seems woven into the fabric of the Time Stream. I tear my eyes away from the blazing illumination, grab Maya and tumble into the oscillating waves.

What is happening to us? Whose time line is that? So many questions. Perhaps the Answer is too much at the moment. Perhaps the Truth is overwhelming.

* * *

Apophis is still going by the name of Apep. Is that his alter ego? Is that how he stalks his prey? Is he lulling the sun-god into a false sense of security in order to acquire advanced knowledge and technology? At what point will he reveal his true nature?

After all the frenetic chasing at the beginning of this adventure I never dreamed I would be spending years on another planet, immersed in politics, military strategy, meditation and art. I have gradually warmed to these humans and increased my level of interaction. Humankind shows great potential and I have high hopes for them.

Maya has acclimatised to Earth and appears to consider it her second home. Although she has made a close friend of Baset, her deepest connection has been forged with the natural environment. She has expanded her repertoire beyond dance and music, travelling across the planet and learning to master the elementals. She seems rather protective of Earth and often has quiet telepathic conversations with plants, trees, animals and birds.

It has been difficult to spend time with Ra because of his involvement with Apophis. Also, Maya and I have refused to partner in the human development initiative, preferring to keep to ourselves. The motto 'Interference is Perilous' has been our guiding light, a piece of wisdom that Arcturians accrued from millennia of experience. Perhaps our behaviour is hypocritical considering the numerous times we have shared our knowledge of the future.

One rare afternoon Ra summons me to his temple. He is concerned about the behaviour of the being known as Apep. Reports have been coming in, claiming that members of his entourage have begun systematically oppressing and dominating the native population. The sun-god seeks my counsel.

Raising my hands. "I did warn you. Why are you asking my advice now?"

*Each being must prove its virtue. Baset has spent much time with Maya. The gods of light have watched you from afar.*

"Did you say 'gods'?"

*You think I walk alone?*

"No ... you have Baset."

*The gods of light are positioned as leaders and teachers across Egypt. Apep has met most of them. He has made a good impression ... with all but one.*

A shimmering woman emerges from the shadows. *This is Isis, goddess and seer.*

I bow respectfully. "Do you mean Light Seer?"

Ra looks at me strangely. *She has visions of the future. What is a Light Seer?*

My brow creases. Ra has immense knowledge and powerful technology, but I come from a world evolved over tens of thousands of years.

"Every galaxy has a Light Seer who is connected to the Universal Council of Light. The Light Seer monitors and reports the movement of consciousness toward the Light. On a more pragmatic level she also updates the Council about the condition of the Time Lord."

*The Time Lord?*

"Yep. An awesomely responsible position."

*Where is the Time Lord located?*

"At the crystal Temple of Arcturus which houses the Galactic Government. On the planet Mani. My home that was destroyed. Hence, my mission."

Ra shifts uncomfortably. Perhaps he now realises that the fate of the galaxy is at stake.

*Isis sees a dark cloud around Apep. She believes he will turn on us and try to subjugate this world.*

"His real name is Apophis, as you will soon discover. He seeks to destroy the original incarnation of the Time Lord. A loop in the time line shows that he resides in Egypt. He must be protected at all costs."

The sun-god is staring at the ground. It seems I may finally have gotten through to him.

*How do we find this Time Lord?*

"I don't know. He is secretive, reclusive and has vast strategic experience."

Ra clamps his fingers in his mouth and whistles loudly. Baset comes scampering in and glares at him. Her back arches and she begins hissing.

*Sorry. It's important.*

"What can Baset do?"

*The Eye of Ra.*

"Yes … and ...?"

*Her all-seeing eye perceives everything, everywhere, in every dimension.*

"In every dimension?"

*Baset is not limited in the same way as us.*

"Ah."

The high-pitched screech startles me.

*Do you know the Artisan? Baset says your energies are intertwined.*

"Yes, of course. I am his apprentice."

Ra smiles wryly. *It's the only anomalous energy in Egypt. Could it be him?*

Words disappear from my mouth. Is it possible? Wasn't our meeting a coincidence? Or is this the enigmatic grand plan that Maya mentioned?

"Have you met the Artisan?"

*I commissioned him to sculpt these statues.*

My mind is reeling at the connections. How does this work? Who's really in charge?

The words of the potter spill into my mind: "Creation and Creator. Flow occurs when these Wills align. The clay needs to surrender to the potter's lofty perspective and sage experience. The potter needs to honour the song within the clay. An intimate conversation is required."

What am I missing? Why is this such a puzzle?

Ra signals to Baset. *Fetch the Artisan. Bring all his equipment and craftwork.*

"You're sending a cat?"

*Egyptian Maus have a top speed of 58 km/h. Baset is even faster. She is probably already there.*

He nods to Isis. *Assemble the gods of light.*

Things are suddenly heating up. My energy tingles with a sense of impending doom. What is the matter with me?

I stroll across the courtyard and repose against a tall obelisk. I have no idea what is going to happen. Where on earth is Maya?

Frightening explosion in the sky. Glance upward. An energy field flickers then falters, revealing a rapidly disintegrating Grey ship. Uh oh. That can't be good.

Isis returns. Ra's countenance pales slightly.

*You were right. He has renamed himself Apophis, proclaimed himself the god of darkness, and is demanding to be worshipped. He has taken the form of a tall dark lizard.*

The words fall from my ears. My heart is racing. Where is Maya?

Chaos descends. Baset arrives with the Artisan. Two labourers are hauling a large wooden cart. Five shining beings appear and hurriedly confer with Ra. The Mau is instructed to stay and protect us. Within moments the gods take their leave.

A war in the heavens ensues. The full extent of the gods' power and presence is felt throughout Egypt and across neighbouring countries. Baset is scanning the battle and reporting critical events to me. Two Grey ships are obliterated. Maya is finally located, her sleek ship manoeuvring deftly through the sky. A fierce boom resounds and a light-ship descends haphazardly to the ground.

A dark beam streaks thunderously across the courtyard, blasting an obelisk into pieces. The Artisan runs out, waving his hands and shouting obscenities. Two Greys materialise near one of the statues. Instantly on my feet … running … everything slowing … "Cronus, wait!" … turning, shocked expression … weapon fire … falling … a blurring through the air … ferocious high-pitched screech … fierce tangle of claws and fangs … enemies down … reach the Artisan … still breathing … *Who are you? How do you know me?* … blood pouring from his chest … shaking my head … trying to stop the bleeding … "I'm on your side … from the future … is this your first incarnation?" … smiling … *No* … another blast … flung through the air … stunned … on my back … the Battleship … Ra's enormous golden spacecraft comes into view … blue undulating waves … Apophis is making the jump … along with five Grey ships … blackness …

"Hey, you ok?"

"Maya! What happened?"

"Your energy shield took the brunt. The Artisan is dead. Battle's over."

Tears fill my eyes. What have I done? How will I explain this to her? Cronus has been killed right in front of me. I stumble over to view the body. Nothing. Complete obliteration. No time to transfer his consciousness.

I walk out the courtyard and down to the river. My eyes are stinging. What use is all the peace and love in me when I can't even save one Time Lord? Apophis has escaped and the chase is on again. I feel totally helpless, utterly useless.

A few hours later I compose myself and trudge back to the temple. My body is aching and my spirit is tender. Ra hails me. He is sitting with Maya finishing what appears to be an intense conversation. She looks me directly in the eyes as I approach.

"It's not your fault, Indra. The Dark Lizard killed him, not you."

I stare at my fidgeting hands. "I'm so sorry."

"Come now. My wily father always had a dozen escape routes. Nothing ever caught him off guard."

"Yeah. Perhaps before Apophis." I take a deep breath. "Wait a minute. How did you find out?"

"Ra explained everything. Cronus was living among us the entire time."

Deep sigh. "Your father died in my arms. With his last breath he told me that this was not his first incarnation."

"There you go. Good news."

She seems to be taking it rather well. I suppose, if put into perspective, she never knew the Artisan. She barely interacted with him. In fact, I don't recall them ever speaking.

Maya places her hands on my shoulders. "We're doing the best we can. Surrender and flow."

I nod quietly.

She studies me for a moment. "Do you think he knew our true identities?"

"No. He was shocked when I called him by his name."

"Ah. We can only assume there is some grand plan. That's too much synchronicity to be a mere random event."

Ra beckons us to follow him. In the huge hall stand eight shimmering beings. *Meet the gods of light: Hathor, Shu, Tefnut, Geb, Nut, Osiris, Isis, Seth and Nephthys.*

Hmm ... nine names, eight beings ... who is missing?

We bow respectfully. The gods bow in return.

*I am despatching the gods to spread our advanced teachings throughout the planet. They have been instructed to adopt a local name and identity when arriving in a new country. This should enable them to blend with the populace. Also, their presence will be less obvious should Apophis make a reappearance.*

My foot nudges a loose stone. "Sensible decision."

Baset trundles over and gazes at Ra. *She says you are going to be leaving soon. Your mission is not complete.*

Maya frowns. "Indeed. This time-place is done."

*You have proved yourselves virtuous. There is much we can learn from each other. You will always be welcome in our family.*

Isis steps forward. *I have seen a vision. You two will return to us. It is part of your destiny.*

What can I say? Suitably vague prophecy. Speculation at best. May as well be polite. "Thank you for allowing us to stay. Our allegiance is with the gods of light."

Ra proffers a rare smile. *Your first allegiance is to Light, Love and Truth.*

Somehow those words seem familiar. We bow once more and make our way to the gleaming spacecraft hovering alongside the courtyard wall.

Baset has followed us. She clambers into the arms of Maya and purrs sweetly, nuzzling her nose against Maya's cheek. The Mau stares intense light blue eyes at me, as if to say goodbye, then jumps to the ground and scampers away.

We board Maya's ship and leap into the Time Stream. One chapter closes, another begins. Where to from here? A sudden thought pads into my mind. Weren't Baset's eyes green? I wonder ...

* * *

Apophis is going to struggle. The time line shows that five Greys escaped. His deputies Sek and Mot are positioned behind the Battleship, followed by the pilots of the other saucer-shaped spacecraft. It is far too risky to return to Area 51 because of the fearsome stories that were purveyed about the Light weapon and he certainly has no wish to experience the wrath and power of Ra.

Strangely, he has jumped forward to Earth-time 336 BC. The dark line intersects once again with Cronus but the Time Lord's numerous intermingled loops are confounding. There is no easy way for Apophis to pinpoint his location. I notice there is also a crossing with a human line, that of a man called Alexander III of Macedon.

Maya is standing next to me in Atra Atha. I motion her to come closer. "What do you think this means?"

She studies the line for a while. "Hmm … My father has the ability to transfer his consciousness and take over another body. Personally, I find that notion uncomfortable but he assured me that it is usually temporary and mostly an emergency measure. No harm is done to the host. Do you think the Dark Lizard has a similar ability?"

I shake my head. "Cronus and Apophis are not Arcturians. Your father has been alive for thousands of years and has clearly mastered his deepest essence: pure consciousness. He can move easily between diverse bodies. Apophis, however, is a potent physical-energetic expression of the Nothing; as such, he has no need to transmigrate. Anyway, he can shape-shift to appear as any entity."

"Then he must have adopted another strategy. Perhaps he is choosing to hide his technology and link with powerful leaders in an effort to track down my father."

"Let's have a closer look at the line of Alexander III of Macedon."

"Olympias is his mother … conception occurs … she has a vivid dream that her womb is struck by a thunderbolt, causing a raging fire that devours the surrounding lands … Alexander is born in 356 BC in Pella, capital of the kingdom of Macedon, a state in northern ancient Greece … at age 13 he begins to be tutored by Aristotle in the disciplines of medicine, philosophy, logic, morals and art … father Philip assassinated in 336 BC … Alexander proclaimed king by the nobles and army at age 20 …"

My brow furrows. "Smells suspicious. Surely the Dark Lizard is involved."

"Relentless battles and invasions over the next decade ... creates one of the largest empires of the ancient world … mysterious death at age 32 …"

I raise my hand. "That's enough. Apophis is tied to Alexander's line for twelve years. He appears intently focused and busy." Staring into the Immersion. "Your father once told me that it was a mistake to keep chasing."

She nods. "Clearly, that hasn't been working for us."

"What if we enter Earth at a time before Apophis and create some good? Kind of like a counterbalance or pre-emptive strike."

"You mean interfere?"

"We've already broken so many rules. And that dark being brazenly meddles in the affairs of this planet. We can't stand by and watch."

"You do realise that if we ever save our world, we'll either be eulogised as heroes or exiled for breaking the time law?"

A sigh escapes my lips. "We might not live to see either."

Stillness hangs uneasily in the air.

Finally, "Alright, let's do it. What do you have in mind?"

I smile. "Grab that time line. Where did Alexander quit his campaigns?"

"India. The army was battle-weary and homesick. He died soon after in the palace of Nebuchadnezzar II, in Babylon, in 323 BC."

"Hmm … I propose we launch an initiative in India two hundred years earlier."

"You mean an armed conflict?"

I burst into laughter. "No. A peace initiative."

Gazing among the undulating waves. "Let's see ... we need royalty ... around 560 BC ... ah ... this is interesting ... the Solar Dynasty ..."

Maya interjects. "Solar, as in sun?"

"Yes ... the Solar Dynasty in India worships the sun-god ... within that dynasty are Kshatriya which means the ruling and military elite ... two Kshatriya families rule kingdoms on opposite banks of the Rohini river: The Koliyas and Sakyas ..."

"How will that be useful to us?"

"We are going to seed an Arcturian child on Earth. The child will need the protection of a powerful family."

Stunned silence. "Are you serious? That's a radical plan."

"These are radical times. Few people know about the Dark Lizard's rampage through this planet. Even fewer have the knowledge and ability to stop him."

"True."

"You still committed?"

Her stare conveys fierce conviction. "Absolutely."

I grab the relevant time lines. "Here we go ... 565 BC ... the Koliyas are rulers of the Kingdom of Devadaha (in 2007 AD this is called the Rupandehi District of Nepal) ... King Anjana has two sons, Suprabuddha and Dandapani, and a daughter, Pajapati ... now look at this ... the Sakyas are rulers of the Kingdom of Kapilvastu (same name in 2007 AD) ... and King Suddhodana is married to Pajapati ..."

"Ah, the blending of two influential families. Looks promising."

"Indeed. Here is the plan: We will cloud the minds of both families. King Anjana will be convinced that he has another daughter named Maya. You will project a very attractive and fecund female image. King Suddhodana will find you irresistible and make you his second wife. This will secure the necessary protection for our child."

"We going to jump to Devadaha, 565 BC?"

"Oh yeah, baby."

She smiles. "I think you are finally developing a sense of humour."

"Me? You cheeky monkey!" I bite my tongue. Never met anyone so serious.

"Well, what are we waiting for?"

She sets the coordinates and we sail through the Time Stream. It will be good having Maya's ship on Earth; it affords an extra level of security. Our destination: The foot of the Himalaya Mountains, the highest and most massive mountain range on the planet. I take a deep breath. Let's hope this all works out.

* * *

It is strange being on Earth again. Can't seem to get away from this place. Perhaps Maya is right – this is all part of some grand plan. Or maybe it's just the relentless pursuit of a dark being from another galaxy. I wonder if he has destroyed any other worlds. How many galaxies has he jeopardised? Or has he tried and failed?

He certainly seems preoccupied with this planet. Perhaps this is the closest he has come to annihilating a Time Lord. If he has tasted success, he is hardly likely to give up now.

"Helloooo."

"What is it?"

"We have arrived. Where are you?"

"Just thinking about Apophis. Hoping our plan will work. I don't want to spend the rest of my life chasing him."

"I believe each of us will have our day to confront the Dark Lizard. We will stand or fall depending on our choices and actions."

"That's a bit dramatic."

She looks thoughtful. "Don't know where that came from. An intuition ..."

"What kind of climate are we expecting?"

"The Himalaya Mountains prevent the influx of frigid winds from icy northern Asia. North India is generally warm or only mildly chilly."

"Depends if we walk in the shade."

"Touché."

"Too-what?"

She laughs. "You sound like an owl."

"Your energy seems upbeat. What's tickling you?"

"Relieved to be away from Apophis. It'll be a vacation without him."

I heave a sigh. "Yeah."

We make our way to the settlement in Devadaha, arriving at the palace of King Anjana at dusk. Maya is projecting the image of a beautiful Indian woman. I accompany her as bodyguard and aide. A sumptuous banquet is being held, with the entire family and numerous guests in attendance. This provides the perfect opportunity to effectuate a public mind cloud. Hopefully the combination of our two minds will create a long lasting effect.

And just like that, Maya becomes a princess, daughter of the Koliyan king. Our advanced brains easily assimilate the local language and it is not long before we feel settled. It's a different kind of lifestyle, lavish and disciplined, and at times reminds me of home. Kshatriya are well schooled in the military arts and horseback riding. Maya's unusual connection with animals does not go unnoticed and soon she is being mentored by her 'father' in the intricacies of horsemanship. The skill of archery seems more befitting of my role; my days become filled with combat training and target practice. How our lives are changing.

A few months later phase two of our plan comes into operation. Maya is introduced to King Suddhodana at an archery competition at the palace in Kapilvastu. He is smitten immediately. My recently acquired dexterity fails to win any commendations, but I am satisfied; it's impressive progress for a being with only three fingers on each hand. The announcement of the impending marriage of King Suddhodana and Princess Maya is made shortly after the festivities.

In 564 BC I attend the opulent wedding in Kapilvastu. Brightly coloured decorations, dazzling outfits and sparkling jewels grace the spectacular multi-day celebration. Guests are encircled by a cacophony of drum beating, horn blowing and bell ringing, and the sweet smell of incense, while abundant fresh flowers, coconuts and rice make their symbolic nuptial statements. Princess Maya is dressed in a gorgeous red sari heavily embroidered with gold thread, and bedecked in ornate gold jewellery. The ceremony and exchange of vows are romantic and memorable. After the blessings are given and the newlyweds are showered with petals, the guests retire to the dining hall where a magnificent feast awaits. Conviviality resounds long into the night.

We manage to carry off the illusion for a solid year, no mean feat considering the amount of people involved. One afternoon I am walking through the forest with Queen Maya. She has a concerned tone in her voice. "I am unsure how long I can keep this up."

"What's the problem? Is the lifestyle too hard?"

"It's the emotional investment. I am connecting deeply with another being. It's confusing to me and ultimately misleading the king."

"You have to keep your eye on the mission."

"Easy words for someone who shoots arrows all day."

"Fair comment."

She frowns. "We need an exit plan."

I ponder the situation awhile. "You need to feign pregnancy. Cloud the king's mind so he remembers a night of passion. Then shift your image gradually so you appear to be carrying a child. Shortly after giving birth we will fake your death."

Slow nod. "I can live with that."

The wonderful news quickly spreads throughout the kingdoms. Joyful celebration is counterpointed by Maya's cool endurance and her focus on the greater good. Thankfully we will have to play our roles for only a few more months.

During the last weeks of pregnancy we are summoned to the Kingdom of Devadaha. Her 'father' insists that she give birth in her true home and requires that both his daughters return immediately. Obviously that would leave King Suddhodana without his wives. After much debate between the royal families, the horses are loaded and Queen Maya embarks the porter-carried palanquin. The journey begins.

The route is direct and simple. On the way Maya and I engage in fervent and hushed discussions. Leaving one kingdom has played in our favour but enacting a birth in another might prove too difficult. Eventually an idea forms.

At the midpoint of our journey, in the town of Lumbini, Maya insists that we rest for the night. Activating the time-dilation ring, we hail her ship and steal into the Stream. Ra once told me that he had created the gods of light. Maya and I are only able to produce an Arcturian. We need Ra's help to craft Arcturian and human genetics so that our child will blend easily into the local population.

We locate the sun-god just a few minutes after we had previously left him. Ah, the joys of time travel. The confused look on his face is priceless. We explain our predicament and he agrees to assist. On one condition: An opportunity to experience the Time Stream. I shrug with resignation. Why not? We've broken every other rule.

We get to work immediately. Maya had the forethought to bring a scraping of King Suddhodana's genetic material. It seems only fair that he should be a parent. We enter the inner sanctum of the temple. The light inside is blazing and the technology is strange and foreign. Once Maya and I have mated spiritually-energetically, Ra takes over, expertly manipulating the genes, chromosomes and DNA. A few hours later we have a perfect humanoid Arcturian child. Maya bonds with it straight away; it's love at first sight. For me, I am still catching up psychologically and emotionally.

We whisk Ra and the child onto Maya's ship and leap into the Time Stream. As soon as the course is set she leans over and whispers in my ear. "Our child needs an Arcturian name. Any ideas?"

I gaze at his cute little face. Ra has given him deep blue eyes that seem to gaze into eternity. "It's like he is staring directly into the Mystery. I propose we call him Siddhartha, comprised from the words *siddha* which means 'accomplished' or 'perfected' and *artha* which means 'purpose' or 'true sense'."

She nods happily. "Excellent choice. His name will be Siddhartha. We must respectfully include the Sakya family name too: Gautama, comprised from the words *go* which means 'sun' or 'star' or 'rays of light' and *tama* which means 'darkness' or 'night'. As in the light-bringer that dispels darkness."

I hold our baby high in the air. "Siddhartha Gautama, I present you to the world. Hope planet Earth is ready!"

We arrive at Lumbini 563 BC. The time-dilation field will no longer be operational. Anyway, we decide that a dramatic entrance is in order. Maya renders the spacecraft visible and shifts the light waves so that it appears to be a huge white elephant carrying a white lotus flower in its curled trunk. The elephant lands heavily on a grassy mound, startling the sleepy entourage. Guards shout warnings. People are unsure how to react.

A full moon is hanging low in the morning sky. The right side of the elephant opens and Queen Maya emerges with her bodyguard. She walks over to a Sal tree and stands beneath it. Her attendants edge closer. She unfolds the soft white cloth and unveils her newborn child. "Prince Siddhartha Gautama!" I shout proudly. Immediately everyone drops to one knee and offers a minute's respectful silence. Then the cheering and jubilation start.

A few bold soldiers circle the white elephant that descended from the sky. The noise attracts the attention of local townspeople who come running to investigate the commotion. An inquisitive crowd slowly gathers. Suddenly a brilliant light beams from the side of the elephant. Moments later Ra makes a theatrical appearance, his luminous body radiating like an intense sun. It becomes difficult to look upon him.

Stupefied silence. You can sense what the crowd is thinking. Could it be? Has the sun-god deigned to make a rare visit to his people? Have the members of the Solar Dynasty truly been blessed on this day? People fall to the ground in prostration.

A proclamation follows. *Arise! I am Ra. Protect this child with your lives. He is destined for greatness on your world.*

A couple of hours later I return the sun-god to his temple in Egypt. I bow courteously. "Thank you for your help. Until we meet again."

He returns the bow. *And so we shall.*

The following day the entourage continue the journey to Devadaha. Our arrival at the palace is met with devoted revelry. Everyone is in high spirits. A hermit seer known as Asita has travelled from her mountain abode to meet the newborn prince and declares that the child will either become a great king or revered holy man, contingent on the child's exposure to human suffering. As she is leaving, Asita shimmers slightly and winks secretively at me. It's Isis! Amazing. The gods of light evidently live for thousands of years.

Seven days after the birth of Siddhartha, Queen Maya falls mysteriously ill and passes away. The palace enters a period of mourning. Her sister Queen Pajapati is assigned to take over as mother. Rumours abound as to the demise and destination of Maya. Her cortège have witnessed too much to believe our propagated illusion. The idea soon spreads that Maya Devi, as they now call her, has ascended to the Trāyastriṃśa Heaven, a heaven that maintains a close physical connection with Earth.

And so a legend is born.

* * *

Having a child for practical reasons turns out to be rather naive. Maya and I have not only forged an intimate connection by mating, we have also formed a strong emotional attachment to our child. Leaving the planet was necessary because of the strain of maintaining our roles but we are certainly not going to be absent parents.

Queen Pajapati has been briefed about Siddhartha's true nature and understands our need to come and go freely. She has happily accepted the responsibility of primary mother. We have adopted fresh disguises as aide and bodyguard to the queen. No one questions our frequent visitations.

The next few years involve a balancing act. One eye is kept on Apophis and one eye on our child. To some extent we have to step back and let his childhood unfold naturally under the guidance of King Suddhodana and Queen Pajapati. Our role is more about spiritual guidance at the appropriate time and, when he is old enough, helping him understand his background and essence.

Ra seems to have used a predominance of human genetics. We notice that Siddhartha needs to eat and sleep and therefore surmise that he will have a normal human lifespan. However, he possesses extraordinary health, strength and vitality. Under the king's tutelage he soon develops into one of the finest archers in the kingdom and, like his true mother, displays a deep affinity for animals, in particular horses. Perhaps because of the unusual circumstances of Queen Maya's death, or possibly because of the prophecy of Asita, the king shields Siddhartha from religious teachings and knowledge of human suffering.

At age 16, King Suddhodana arranges the marriage of Prince Siddhartha and a young woman named Yasodhara. It is not long before she gives birth to a son, Rahula. The overprotective king provides everything the family wants and desires, ensuring that they never need to leave the bounds of the kingdom. Despite our occasional whispered words of advice, until the age of 28 Siddhartha lives a cloistered and lavish existence filled with every imaginable pleasure. Then at age 29 the Arcturian spirit finally activates. Perhaps Ra had a plan after all.

It starts with an itch that cannot be scratched. A general and increasing dissatisfaction with life as he knows it. Power, wealth and pleasure no longer bring the happiness once experienced. Siddhartha embarks on clandestine trips beyond the palace walls with his servant Chandaka. For the first time he encounters sickness, suffering and ageing, and his world shifts dramatically. How can I judge him? Life on Mani created a similar sheltered existence for me, reducing my awareness of other struggling realities. And that was reinforced by the non-interference rule.

Things escalate rapidly when the prince stumbles upon a diseased man, a decaying corpse and an ascetic all on the same day. Chandaka has to explain that an ascetic abstains from worldly pleasures, usually with the aim of pursuing religious and spiritual goals. Soon after, Siddhartha decides to permanently leave the royal palace. He escapes under cover of a moonless night, accompanied by Chandaka and riding his beloved horse Kanthaka.

Convincing his loyal servant to return to the palace with his horse and belongings, Siddhartha begins a new life as a mendicant, begging for charitable donations. And so his quest to existentially understand the human condition commences in earnest. He spends three years mastering yogic meditation under two hermit teachers and achieves a level of peace but no answers. His next experiment, along with a group of companions, involves deprivation, austerity and self-mortification. After nearly starving himself to death and collapsing in a river, Maya and I step in to provide some guidance.

His mother gently embraces him. "My dear Siddhartha, the physical body has absolutely no relevance to spiritual awakening. Your body is merely an illusion and a projection of consciousness. Neither indulgence nor asceticism will further your spiritual goals. Take care of your health and focus your mind inward, for that is where the answers are to be found."

"Maya Devi, meditation has proven unsatisfactory."

"Meditation is not about achievement. It is about witnessing. Learn to become the observer of your thoughts and emotions. Notice internal and external events. In time you will discover the being that observes. Mindfulness leads to your true nature – pure consciousness."

He nods. "Nothing to do. Nothing to accomplish. Be the mindful observer."

Maya smiles. "There are a few shortcuts too. Take that Bodhi tree, for example."

"The Sacred Fig? The one with the heart-shaped leaves?"

"Yes. Try meditating under that."

"Why?"

"Trust me. The best secrets are experienced and not easily shared."

A frown creases my forehead. What on earth is she talking about?

She laughs cheerfully. "This wondrous planet has buried its gateways to the Mystery in plain sight. Nature harbours delicious secrets. Open your eyes and discover the keys."

I have no idea. Hope our son can make sense of it. We turn and walk away, leaving him alone with his thoughts.

Whatever Maya was conveying, her instruction certainly has a profound effect. Siddhartha seats himself under the Sacred Fig and vows never to arise until he has found the Truth. That action only makes me feel more concerned. This is heightened when his companions desert him, believing that Siddhartha has abandoned his quest.

The Bodhi somehow works a miracle. The word *bodhi* means 'wisdom' and after 49 days of contemplation Siddhartha acquires the deepest insight. Maya gazes upon him from the lofty perch of Atra Atha. "Your son is now awakened. He has attained enlightenment. Henceforth he will be known as the Buddha, which means one who is 'wise, awakened and enlightened'."

Shaking my head. I need to understand what has happened. "Let me spend some time alone with him. There are many questions troubling me."

She acquiesces immediately. "Yes. I think that would be good for you."

I leave the Time Stream and stroll over to my 35-year-old son, then bow respectfully and sit at his feet. "Gautama Buddha. Teach me. Give me the Answer. What have you attained?"

Siddhartha laughs joyfully. "Nothing. Whatsoever I have attained was already inside me. It is not something new that I have achieved. I have encountered my eternal nature – pure consciousness. I was not mindful about it, I was not aware of it. The treasure was always here, but I had forgotten about it."

"Tell me about the nature of suffering."

"Ah. The Four Noble Truths."

I look at him quizzically.

"First Noble Truth. Suffering, anxiety, frustration and dissatisfaction result from the fact that each one of us is growing old, getting ill and eventually dying. Also from the realisation that all life forms are impermanent, constantly changing and uncontrollable. Each person stares directly into this existential crisis, though many choose to ignore it or pretend it does not exist."

I nod. That inescapable truth burdens every living being.

"Second Noble Truth. The body-mind craves the avoidance of pain, the pursuit of pleasure and the actualisation of identity. These are foolish distractions that draw attention away from the existential crisis. We fear experiencing what we don't want or not obtaining what we do want; we hunt a multitude of pleasures and desperately attach to them; we try to become somebody and chase praise and recognition to bolster the idea of the special self."

Ok, I accept those ideas. Everything makes sense so far.

"Third Noble Truth. Each person needs to understand that existential suffering can cease. That life can be lived fully and freely, in the moment, in the awareness of one's own divine Consciousness."

Losing me now. How can suffering simply cease? What does that mean?

"Fourth Noble Truth. Everything you seek is hidden within you. Although various stepping stones exist for you to discover your deepest essence, the stones are not the Answer. The risk is that people will focus on the path instead of the destination."

"Gautama Buddha, what is the destination?"

He smiles kindly. "You."

"And what is the path?"

A sage countenance. "You want me to outline a path? Meditation gave me a certain peace but it did not awaken me. Harming or indulging my body proved irrelevant. Enlightenment has nothing to do with the body-mind. I awakened within 49 days. How can I prescribe a path?"

"I don't understand. What will you teach people?"

"The Buddha cannot teach enlightenment. Equally, enlightenment is not something you attain. I have shared with you my *arya satya* which means 'noble truths'. However, these are not teachings but my own experiences. How do I translate the Divine into mundane guidelines?"

I heave a sigh.

"The way is not without but within. Where do you want me to point? Enlightenment is an experience of the Divine. It is the sinking and submerging of the illusory self into the Lake of Light until you are aware only of Consciousness. You are Consciousness. Everything is Consciousness and everything is a manifestation of the Source. Except for the Nothing, but that is a whole other subject."

My body starts tingling. Familiar territory. Maybe here is something I can grasp. "Suffering ceases when you encounter the Divine?"

"Existential suffering ceases when you realise that you *are* the Divine. That you are not separate from All That Is. Suffering is the result of believing in the illusory self. Separate 'you' does not exist; only Divine You exists. All Life is the flow of Divine You."

"And what happens when you drown in the Lake of Light?"

"You realise who you are. You discover your true nature. And your mundane life automatically right-sides."

"Right-sides?"

Siddhartha raises his palms. "What is within reflects without. The shell of this body-mind still exists but I Am the Source. This manifestation was lopsided and walking askew through earthly life, leaving chaotic footprints and cycles of unease and unhappiness. Now this being is right-sided and walks with right vision, right intention, right speech, right action, right livelihood, right effort, right mindfulness and right concentration."

"I knew it! There is a Way. An Eightfold Path."

"Indra, take great care. Enlightenment is a profound and enduring *experience*. It is not the result of ethical actions. You cannot earn or achieve it. If you publish any kind of Path, there is the danger of prescriptions or religious ordinances. People tend to become disciples and blindly follow rites, rituals and ceremonies in a misguided attempt to capture an *event*."

"Oh, I see ..."

He looks sternly at me. "Slap my face, hard."

"No."

"Just do it!" he shouts.

I whack my palm against his cheek. It reddens immediately. "Sorry. Does it hurt?"

"What do you think?"

"It looks painful."

He smiles gleefully. "The shell of my conditioned body-mind still exists. If you assail my body, there will be pain. If I lose someone I love, I will grieve. This is the fun of illusory duality. I know I

Am. Yet I find myself still expressed in this limited reality. Part human, part divine."

Sudden flash of insight. "Wait a minute. Isn't it all a choice?"

"Indeed. As long as I hold onto this sliver of personal consciousness, as long as that remains, I do not fully dissolve into the Light. That is my choice. One I make every moment."

"What would happen if you let go?"

"I would disappear from your reality. In fact, I would disappear from all realities. I would be the Source, the underlying unmanifested Is-ness."

"Wow. That's a lot to consider."

"Yes, but you can handle it. You've come this far. Every seeker needs advanced lessons once in a while."

We burst into laughter.

"Have you read these?" He hands me a stack of neatly rolled manuscripts. "It's called the Rigveda which means 'verses of knowledge'."

"No. What is it?"

"One of the mechanisms of Truth on this Earth."

"Where did it originate?"

"Now there's a question. Existing for over a thousand years, the Rigvedic hymns are dedicated to various deities, chiefly the heroic god Indra whose actions led to the destruction of Vrtra, the Dark Lizard."

"Really?" I ask incredulously.

"Yes, really. It also expounds the Agni, or sacrificial fire, and Soma, the sacred drink and the plant from which it is made."

"What is Agni?"

He smiles again. "Agni is the fire that consumes the self."

"What fire?"

"Love, of course."

"Love is a fire?"

His blue eyes seem to penetrate my core. "There are only two paths to enlightenment: Love and Awareness."

"So there are paths?"

"View them as ongoing dedicated experiences. Agni is the fire that consumes you. The more you truly love, the more you die to self. Love is therefore a path to enlightenment."

"And Soma?"

Jovial laughter erupts. "Soma is the water that consumes the self. The crystal clear shimmer of awareness."

I sigh. "You lost me again."

"Give me the manuscripts." Brief silence. "Rigveda 8.48.3 says *ápāma sómam amŕtā abhūmâganma jyótir ávidāma devân* which translates as '... drank Soma ... became immortal ... experienced the Light ... discovered the gods ...'"

"Wow."

Siddhartha points to a document. "The Ninth Mandala of the Rigveda is known as the Soma Mandala. It is all about the purified drink Soma which is made by pounding the Soma plant and filtering the juice through lamb's wool. In fact, the word Soma means 'nectar of heaven' and the Rigveda refers to it as Plant of the Gods."

"Fascinating."

"Indeed."

His blue eyes light up. He leans forward conspiratorially. "Do you see those yellow plants growing around the Sacred Fig?"

"The ones with the long stalks?"

Eyebrows raising. "Yes. Those ones."

I gaze upon the swaying plants. "49 days?"

A smile dances across his face. Slight nod. "More than enough time."

The sun glimmers its sparkling rays over the lush vegetation. A gentle breeze caresses the water lilies in the shining lake. A stunning red lotus catches my attention. I take a deep breath and absorb the surrounding natural beauty. Eventually I sit beneath the Sacred Fig and close my eyes. It's been a cryptic conversation and there is much to ponder.

* * *

I spend the next few weeks with my son on Earth. Apart from my constant endeavours to unravel the enigmatic experiences of the Buddha, I am also studiously watching the growing number of followers that his inner light seems to be attracting.

At first Siddhartha refuses to teach, saying that there is nothing to share and nothing to do. He appears to function in continual bliss and expresses no interest in anything or anyone. I am beginning to understand why awakened beings disappear into caves and forests, becoming uncommunicative hermits.

"How can I teach about an experience?" he says one day. "Every word my mouth forms is a deplorable description of the Divine; every sentence fails miserably to explain the Mystery. Enlightenment is not a process; it is not the result of righteous practices; it is an event. It is the irrevocable shifting of consciousness. It can happen in 49 seconds, 49 years or 49 lifetimes. Even that description is pointless because I exist in the eternal Here Now."

It is interesting to observe initial encounters with Gautama Buddha. Many people are naturally drawn to the I Am light that radiates from his being. They seek to know what he possesses, to understand his deep serenity, to sit at his feet and bask in the abundant joy. A few seem instantly repelled and quickly become critical and angry; others proceed to spread slanderous rumours.

It's always surprising to see the negative reactions, considering that the Buddha is just being. Why should it irk people? Why do they become so upset?

I ask him about this during a private moment. He shrugs. "The Light is the Light. Those who are ready are drawn toward it. They seek the awakening. There are also those whose psychological and emotional wounds are too great, whose earthly minds are too jaded, whose ego attachments are too strong, and those whose spirits swirl with dark energy. Such people find the Light unbearable, even painful. Their only recourse is to hide or try to destroy the Light."

"That's sad."

"It is what it is. No being can escape their own salvation. No being can avoid personal responsibility. Each person treads the path of their choosing. Some take the long circuitous route but they all get here in the end."

"There must be a way to help them."

He smiles patiently. "What would you have me do? Tone down the Light? Not be awakened? Chase after detractors and try to convince them? Take away their personal responsibility?"

"Deep inside, they must feel lonely and empty."

"Indeed. The further they move from the Source, the greater their isolation and suffering."

I interlace my fingers thoughtfully. "So … what can we do?"

"Love is patient and kind. It rejoices in the truth. It is courageous, compassionate and forgiving. It encourages responsibility and service."

"Ah …"

The Buddha slowly blinks.

"Indra, you are a cunning and wise man. I need to leave the mountaintop and teach those in the valleys."

I nod gently.

"How shall I teach what cannot be taught? How shall I render the ineffable Divine into common understanding?"

"My son, words are just seeds. Share your knowledge by way of stories, allegories and parables. Each person will understand the story on some level. Each person will hear what they are ready to hear. The seeds may only sprout in a few weeks' or even a few years' time. But it's not about the story. It's about the transmission of enlightened energy so the soil becomes fertile and the seeds can grow."

Siddhartha bows deferentially. "My deepest gratitude, father."

I step closer and give him a boisterous hug.

Over the next few months Gautama Buddha travels throughout northeast India, sowing parables and spreading the Light. Maya and I watch him from Atra Atha and marvel at his progress. He has naturally attracted a cluster of devotees and people flock around him wherever he goes. He seems to be handling it rather well.

One day Siddhartha is sitting by a gushing river. On the opposite bank a man is standing perplexed. Eventually he waves and shouts "Great Master, I have journeyed many hours to meet you. How can I reach the other side?"

The Buddha bursts into his characteristic jovial laughter. Then he shouts back "My friend, you are already on the other side!" Instantly the man is awakened and hurries back to his village.

We are gazing at the Immersion. A moment of alarm. Dark line intertwining with Siddhartha. We quickly trace it. Of the five Greys that escaped with Apophis, one has been sent back to investigate Gautama Buddha. His name is Mara and we have little information about him. We activate our bracelets and head to Earth.

Soon that familiar saucer-shaped craft appears. The mauve stone on the bracelet temporarily disrupts the incoming waves, rendering the ship visible. It hovers briefly in the distance then flits into the hills. The next day a stranger arrives at the community. Calling himself Devadatta, he quietly takes a seat and listens to the stories of the Buddha.

Only Maya and I know the stranger's true identity. We watch him closely. Nothing much happens. A few days pass. Then it begins. Warming up with surly comments and disrespectful remarks, he soon graduates to direct challenges. Evidently his goal is to undermine the Buddha and cast doubt into the minds of his followers. Finally, a veiled threat: "If you are the Divine then no harm shall come to you. You will always be protected. However, if you fall to the ground, all shall know you as a fraud."

The Buddha smiles and says "Believe nothing, no matter where you read it, no matter where you heard it. Ignore even my words, unless they accord with your own soul and your own experience. The path is within not without."

Early one morning a huge boulder rolls down the hill, narrowly missing our son. Thankfully no one is injured. The following week a drunk elephant stumbles into the throng. Siddhartha waves his hand in amusement. "Even the animals seek my counsel." His natural affinity for wildlife is obviously unknown to the Grey. The elephant simply collapses at the Buddha's feet. Laughter peals through the crowd.

A fortnight later a group of archers ambush the community. Gautama Buddha ignores them and carries on with one of his parables. "A beggar woman lights her oil lamp and leaves it on the temple steps. She does this so that the monks can find their way. In the night a terrible storm soaks the surrounding forest. Darkness besets the temple. The storm turns into a typhoon. Soon dozens of villagers are stumbling up the sacred steps to find shelter. Fear ripples through the huddled mass. Strangely, the wick of the beggar's lamp remains as new and the oil stays full, providing comfort and guidance during the ensuing nights. The light is never extinguished."

The ambience changes dramatically. The crowd senses it. One by one, the archers lay down their bows and beg forgiveness. They are immediately welcomed into the community. It's too much for Devadatta. He steps forward and confronts Siddhartha. "You are a fraud and liar. You offer a Way to nothing, a Path to nowhere. These people are blind and gullible. It is my duty to destroy you."

I move to protect my son but Maya grabs my arm. "Wait a little. Let's see what happens. We can't always be here to protect him."

The Buddha pulls out his secret weapon. Jovial laughter reverberates along the mountains and sweeps into the valley. The crowd falls apart in mirth and merriment. The laughter is neither mocking nor critical. It is the pure joy of Existence, resounding across the ages and penetrating even the deepest darkness. Mara the Grey desperately tries to close his ears. He seems torn by conflicting energies. Who can possibly withstand the onslaught of such euphoria?

The laughter continues for another half-hour. It is a powerful and profound experience. Some devotees are rolling on the ground; others are crying streams of tears. Suddenly a collective sigh. Everything quietens. The Buddha looks directly at Mara and says "Thousands of candles can be lit from a single candle, and the life of the candle will not be shortened. You cannot prevent the sharing of Light, Love and Peace. Darkness will never extinguish the Light."

The Grey's face seems to crumple. He turns on his heel and takes flight. I smile at Maya. "Apophis is going to discover a new chink in his armour. It will be difficult to protect that weakness."

It is time to leave Siddhartha. As much as we love him, we've got a planet to save. The altercation with the Grey has reminded us of our mission. As long as the Dark Lizard is alive, everything is under threat. We have to consider more than ourselves.

We arrange a private meeting with our son. The hugs are intense, the farewell emotional. He knows we are proud of him and that we are never far away. A blue portal shimmers nearby. We make the jump. My heart feels heavy. Saying goodbye to another loved one. I sigh and turn the key to enter Atra Atha.

* * *

Maya and I are quite morose. Neither of us is great company. Our return to the Time Stream is synchronous with Apophis' next move. Before the pursuit begins, we steal a glance at Siddhartha's time line. He lives for 80 years, finishing his life in 483 BC in Kushinagar, India. He has managed to spread a considerable amount of Light and the Stream reflects a multitude of positive ripples. The information warms our hearts and draws us out of the sullen mood.

It looks like the Dark Lizard has given up with Earth. Perhaps he is tired of chasing the ghost that is Cronus. Or maybe his forces have taken too many hits. I am watching with fascination as his dark line proceeds.

I shout across to Maya. "You won't believe this. He is returning to Mani. Two hundred years before the destruction of the Arcturian planets."

She strolls into the Immersion. "Uh oh. That's not good."

"Why? What do you mean?"

Taps her head. "Hello. When were you born? When was I born?"

"Oh my ..."

"Exactly. If we are never created, it reverses everything we have achieved on Earth."

"Wow." I have to admire Apophis. He is a relentless and devious strategist.

"What are we going to do? He has six spacecraft that have been adapted to time travel and five Greys capable of image projection."

"Yeah, but there are two of us." I burst into laughter. Where did that come from? Must be a residual effect of spending time with Siddhartha.

"Keep an eye on him. Tell me when and where to make the jump."

"Are we travelling in your ship?"

"Of course. Did you think I was going to park it here?"

"No. Just checking."

Phew. Seems the quick-tempered Maya is back. It gets rather tiresome. Hope she loosens up someday.

"Well?"

I point to the relevant time-place. "Uh … he has despatched Mara to our birthplace … but Apophis is mingling with our adult time lines …"

"We have to make a choice."

"The birthplace is a natural priority. Let's jump."

It turns out that Maya is the same age as me. And we grew up in the same sector. Young Arcturians spend the majority of their days under the care of professional childminders. Our socialisation and education start at an early age. Mara the Grey is making his way to our playschool.

We arrive a little earlier and scout the premises. Our bracelets will ensure that we can penetrate the image that Mara will be projecting. It is not long before a kind-looking Arcturian appears in the playground outside the school. It's him. We stroll over and bow respectfully, pretending to be security officers.

"Greetings, friend. How may we help you?"

"Substitute childminder. Just for today."

"May we scan your energy to ascertain your identity?"

"Uh ... no ..." He pulls a weapon from his cloak.

Ah. We have an uncomfortable stand-off. Where's the Vajra when you need it?

I rub my chin. "Is that some sort of identity card?"

He waves the weapon menacingly. A normal Arcturian would have panicked by now. After all, weapons are banned on Mani. No one sees them. But a lot has happened to me. I can't help myself. I fall into a fit of unbridled laughter.

Maya gapes at my unnatural behaviour. I can't seem to control it. The laughter gets louder and more raucous. A couple of passers-by get the giggles. Maya's face creases into a broad smile and her lip starts quivering. The Grey looks nervous. After fifteen minutes, silence suddenly envelops us.

I stare into Mara's eyes. "By the way, Gautama Buddha sends his regards." Laughter grips me once more. It's the tipping point. The capitulation of darkness in the face of supreme positive energy. The Grey drops the weapon and apologises. Unbelievable. I smile to myself. Perhaps I have developed a psychoSomatic condition. Slapping my thigh at the private joke. No point sharing it with Maya.

Her hand grips my shoulder. "Indra, pull yourself together. I have an idea." She motions to the Grey. "Apophis must have escorted you here. The Cosmic Shield would have denied access to a foreign spacecraft. If you want your freedom, follow us."

We walk to a nearby field then board Maya's ship and hover in the Time Stream. "Set course for Earth. Area 51, 1979."

I look at her quizzically. "Why there?"

Fierce glare. "Trust me."

She hurriedly scans a time line then whispers into my ear. "Cronus is still in the body of a Grey. He has become their leader. Obviously they do not know his true identity."

"Ah …"

We arrive at the portal in the Stream. "You need to stay with the ship. I am going to deliver the Grey to his people on Earth. They are no longer slaves of Apophis."

"Uh … Will the leader know you?"

"Hope so. I'll mention your name."

"Right ..."

"See you in a while."

"Don't take too long. We have that other pressing matter."

Brief nod. They jump through the portal. All I can do is wait.

Maya soon returns, big smile on her face.

"Hey, everything go well?"

"Yeah. It's the first time he has met me. Isn't that weird? He still has to create me in the future."

"Let's hope he doesn't change his mind."

"Very funny."

"Update me. What's been happening on Earth?"

She sits in the captain's chair. "Those Greys are an unruly bunch. With Apophis gone, they don't care for rules or authority. Like all beings they want to be free and independent. Cronus has his hands full trying to lead them."

"What is their function now?"

"You're going to need the backstory."

"I'm listening ..."

Deep breath. "Majestic-12 has become a powerful secret international organisation, no longer merely serving America's interests. It controls a consortium of political, military and economic assets. The organisation has a new name and its ruling elite have big plans for the planet."

"How interesting."

"They have two priorities: One, institute a planetary defence system to protect against alien invasion; two, create a new world order to rule the planet. Area 51 and similar bases around the globe report directly to the organisation. The Greys are trading their advanced knowledge for the right to propagate their species."

"I need more details."

"The Greys provide knowledge and support to meet the two priorities. In exchange, they seek to improve their cloning abilities. Apophis took the cloning technology with him. They are therefore a dying race. The elite have given the Greys permission to abduct humans and carry out genetic experiments, including human-alien hybridisation."

"We are hardly in a position to judge such behaviour."

She looks at me disapprovingly. "We don't abduct people."

"True."

"Oh … Cronus said we might need this."

I glance at the screen. "What is it?"

"The genetic code of the Greys."

"Hmm … it may be useful one day."

"Earth's planetary defence system is about to go live. The public will only be told about it in a few years' time. Its true purpose will remain hidden. The military are calling it the Star Wars programme."

"A very sensible strategy. Especially if Apophis ever chooses to return to Earth. He would have to infiltrate positions of power and deactivate the defence system before summoning his ships."

Maya and I stare at each other. My forehead creases. "Are you thinking what I'm thinking?"

"The Cosmic Shield?"

"Yes! That must be how Apophis did it. Infiltrated Mani, got the code, deactivated the shield. And that's why our enemy was invisible. Disguised spacecraft, shape-shifting Dark Lizard and image-projecting Greys."

"Apophis only has four Greys with him now."

"Then he must have cloned an army before the attack. He obliterated all the Arcturian planets after Mani was destroyed."

Maya blinks rapidly. "Aren't you in charge of the Cosmic Shield? How many people know the code?"

"An energy-field scan grants only three people, including me, access to a randomised and ever-changing code. It is valid for 60 seconds."

"Who are the other two?"

"For each planet: The President and the Technology Leader. That is why we seldom leave our planets. However, on Mani, because the Galactic Government is situated there, we have a third person: Galactic Leader Savitri."

She gazes at me. "There's a weak link somewhere."

We park the ship and enter Atra Atha. Walk into the Immersion. Our time lines are flickering wildly. Apophis!

"Maya, our adult lives! He is intersecting rapidly. Something is happening."

"Oh no. It's too late!"

"It's never too late." I grab her arm and launch us through the Time Stream. How could Apophis attack the two of us together? We've not met before.

We burst through the glowing door. It's an academic conference. People have finished for the day and are bustling into the recreation hall. It's busy and telepathic conversations abound. There I am, back to the wall, chatting with a colleague. On the other side of a high table is Maya. We don't know each other.

"Cloud your younger version's mind and push her into that room. Then take her place at the table. I will take care of mine."

"What?"

"Just do it!"

The whole thing takes three minutes. I am now chatting with my colleague. It's rather bizarre. No idea what's going to happen. I scan the room. One of the professors strides over. I remember his excellent lecture and bow respectfully. He uncharacteristically embraces me and the knife slips unseen into my chest. My knees buckle. The room is spinning. Maya is looking in the wrong direction. I try to call out but helplessly watch her suffer a similar fate. Everything becomes dark.

* * *

Swirling mist. Rapid cascading images. Feeling of being sucked through a vortex. Jumbled roaring sound. Blurry reflections. Arrive with a jolt. Sudden sharp focus.

"What the –"

She sits in the captain's chair. "Those Greys are an unruly bunch. With Apophis gone, they don't care for rules or authority. Like all beings they want to be free and independent. Cronus has his hands full trying to lead them."

"Wait. You've told me that before."

"I have. What's going on?"

"We went to Earth and traded places with our younger selves. Remember?"

"I do."

"Apophis killed us."

"Why aren't we dead?"

I rub my chin. "Our younger versions lived. Their time lines must have continued exactly as before. Apophis still destroys our planets. It's one big circle."

"That scrambles my mind. Are we still the same people?"

"Apparently."

"I don't feel different."

"If Apophis had killed our younger selves, we'd be dead."

We park the ship and enter Atra Atha. Walk into the Immersion. Our time lines are flickering wildly. Apophis!

"Oh no! It's the same event! What are we going to do?"

We leap through the Stream again. Cloud the minds of our younger selves. Barely have time to take our positions. Galactic Leader Savitri approaches. I bow respectfully. The knife slips unseen. Maya struggles briefly. Everything turns black.

Swirling images. Rush of noise. Shudder. Shake my head. Regain focus.

Maya is shouting. "What's happening? Please make it stop!"

Apophis is repeatedly trying to kill us. It must be a critical event. Why now? Why here?

The academic conference took place *after* the Dark Lizard's arrival in this galaxy. And *after* the interactions with Priya. What am I missing? He must have traded information. Maya invited Priya into the Time Chamber because she possessed uncommon information about the operation of the Time Stream. My wife … seduced by power and ambition … traded knowledge … about her husband the Technology Leader …

We park the ship and enter Atra Atha. Walk into the Immersion. Our time lines are flickering wildly. Apophis!

No choice. Leap through the Stream again. Burst into the recreation hall. Cloud the minds of our younger selves. Push them into the small room. Prepare to be ambushed. That can't be

Cronus! Is it him? Maya melts into his arms and begs for help. The knife slips unseen. I resist as long as possible but flounder under the strength of the Dark Lizard.

Roaring cascade. Quicker than last time. Shudder. Arrive. Regain my composure.

Need to use the time more effectively. Grab her arm. Step into Atra Atha. Dash into the Immersion. What happens after Apophis obtains the key from Priya? They become invisible. Must have stepped into the other galaxy. No record of the transaction. The next move is Apophis' jump into the past. But I know that already. That's how the chase began.

Wait. That cunning lizard had a time-dilation ring. Could there be some missing time? I refine the search parameters. There it is! Squeezed into the briefest moment, an entire event. It's Priya ... no, her time line has ended ... it's a shape-shifted illusion of Priya ... sneaking out of the visible time line ... meets her husband briefly after he returns from visiting an outpost ... I remember this! ... in my office at the Pagoda ... planned maintenance of the Cosmic Shield ... have to say goodbye ... she walks away ... aha! ... dials the ring ... watches me access the code ... inputs it immediately into another terminal ... creates an override authority ... oh my ... it's me! ... I am the one who accidentally betrayed the code ... caused the shield to come down ...

"Indra! It's happening again!"

Filled with fear, anxiety and frustration. Leap through the Time Stream. Burst into the recreation hall. Cloud the minds of our younger selves. Need to break this loop. Think! Bundle all four of us toward the glowing blue door. Insert the key. Turn it right. Step into blazing light.

We are shielding our eyes. None of us can see. Where are we?

"Indra?"

"Maya, I have no idea."

Our younger selves remain under the influence of the mind cloud. Calm, unquestioning, unreactive. They will not remember these bizarre events.

"What did you do?"

I shrug and raise my hands. "Same thing I always do. Insert the key and turn."

It's quiet for a while.

"You must have done something different."

Retracing the hectic activity … entered through the same door …

"Which direction did you turn the key?"

"Um … to the right."

"Are you sure?"

"Uh … yes."

"We always turn Time Keys to the left. As you well know."

She's correct. Cronus gave me that specific instruction. Never thought much about it. Became an automatic behaviour. Why on earth did I turn the key to the right? "Are we in trouble now?"

"How would I know? I've never turned a key the wrong way."

I heave a sigh.

"Hey, can you feel a presence? A kind of warm and friendly ambience?"

"Yeah." She tries to look around.

My eyes are beginning to adjust. We are completely immersed in golden-white light. No time lines. No portals. No reference points.

"This reminds me of the strange time line we gripped –"

"Was just thinking that. The message about the Nothing and the Something."

I rub the back of my head. "Have we accessed the pure Something?"

"You mean the Source? The underlying Is-ness?"

"Uh … yeah …"

She frowns. "It's beyond me."

"As far as I understand, the Something consists of the unmanifested Consciousness or Source and the multitudinous manifested Realities. Although no division actually exists. It is all Consciousness. It is all Is-ness. It is all Something."

"I should have spent more time with Siddhartha."

"Understanding the Mystery comes from direct experience not the teachings of others."

"Well spoken."

We float in the Light, trying to make sense of our location. Unsure of our ability to move or find direction. Every action produces no result. We are effectively immobilised.

The subtlest shift in energy. The feeling of focused attention. A booming voice resounds in our minds.

**Indra and Maya, what are you doing here?**

I speak first. “Um … we’re kinda lost.”

**Are you now?**

“Uh … yeah.”

Silence prevails.

Glance across at Maya and shrug. Sudden pang of anxiety. “Has Apophis ever turned the key to the right?”

**Numerous times.**

“And …”

**You know the Answer.**

“Nothing is not Something. Darkness is repelled by the Light. He would have felt like he was disintegrating. Too painful.”

**Your wisdom has grown, Indra.**

“Is the Something completely surrounded by the Nothing?”

**Obviously.**

“What is beyond the Nothing?”

Long silence.

I cough uncomfortably.

**I sense the love of One greater than me.**

Wow. My mind is tripping.

"Really? A greater Something?"

**Indeed.**

"Oh. The next level. A whole other dimension."

**More than a dimension. Another level of Being.**

"I can barely grasp that idea. It's enough just trying to understand God."

**You turned the key right for a reason.**

Her voice intercedes. "We are trying to save Arcturus."

**Ah, Maya. You've been quiet.**

"Can you help us?"

**And take away your free will?**

"But there's a divine plan. I know it."

Booming laughter. **Life at every level.**

"Please give us a clue."

**What does Atra Atha mean?**

I rub my chin. "Here Now."

**Usually only Time Lords and Light Seers enter.**

What is God talking about? I suddenly burst into laughter. Soon tears are streaming down my face. The sheer absurdity of it all. I am having a conversation with God, expecting a miraculous Answer. But I am God. I am the Source. I am Light. I am Love.

My mind erupts into streams of Light. My being explodes with Love. My consciousness is overwhelmed with Joy. Indra disappears. I Am! I Am! I Am! I Am. I Am.

Everything stops. I Am. Here. Now. Being.

The words of the Buddha flow into my mind. "As long as I hold onto this sliver of personal consciousness, as long as that remains, I do not fully dissolve into the Light. That is my choice. One I make every moment."

My words to him follow soon after. "Love is patient and kind. It rejoices in the truth. It is courageous, compassionate and forgiving. It encourages responsibility and service."

I stare into the face of God.

Eventually I turn to Maya. "Come with me."

She holds my hand. "Where are we going?"

"We are consciousness and our intention directs our journey."

The Time Stream appears. I usher the four of us into the undulating waves. Carefully insert the Time Key into the door of Atra Atha and turn it left.

I explain what she needs to hear. "Apophis arrives from another galaxy. No allies. No ships. However, he is highly intelligent, knowledgeable and devious. He has accrued a deep understanding of time travel. Priya is seduced by his darkness and obtains a key for this galaxy's Stream. She is eliminated. Apophis then surreptitiously uses his ring to bend time and steal the Cosmic Shield access code, installing a permanent authority in the system. Now he just has to raise a military force.

"To draw attention away from his evil deeds he immediately jumps into the past, but not before ambushing Cronus and seizing the master key. He aims to assemble an army so he ransacks the Pleiades, implementing a time loop which makes it difficult to follow him. We catch up with him and he crashes onto Earth. Somehow he succeeds in building a military force but chooses to leave when Cronus launches the Area 51 attack.

"He runs further into the past, discovers the powerful gods of light and hopes to acquire their technology. Impatience and arrogance drive him into battle with Ra and he pays the price. He limps into the future on Earth trying to uncover Cronus' first incarnation. He has killed Cronus many times but still not achieved his objective of wiping out this galaxy's Time Lord.

"Jumping forward to Arcturus, he sets the stage for his final plan: Get rid of the annoying Technology Leader and Time Lord's daughter; reassemble a military force; destroy the Arcturian planets. All his nefarious actions serve his primary mission: Destroy Time and obliterate the Something.

"The desperate attempt to kill us at the academy reflects a pivotal point. It was crucial to eliminate us. For once, we have successfully interrupted his time line."

Maya speaks. "I don't understand. Why are we so important?"

"Isn't it obvious? We are the only ones who know what he has been doing. We know his thought process and strategy. We can predict his behaviour. We can change the future."

"How?"

"By combining our skills: Technology and Time."

"More details, please."

"Gaze into the Immersion." I point to the Dark Lizard's time line.

"Where is he?"

"Observe. When I turned the key to the right, we effectively disappeared from the Stream. Apophis must have assumed we were deceased. He then departed to assemble the military force required to obliterate the Arcturian planets."

"Why can't we see him?"

"Same reason as last time. He jumped into his old galaxy. Rendering him invisible to us. But …" I wave my finger sagely. "We can predict his next move."

She smiles. "I'm listening."

"Here is the time line of Mani. Apophis will reappear to destroy our world. We move forward … forward … wait for it … there! The Cosmic Shield fails ... infiltration of Greys … reign of invisible terror … annihilation …"

Her hand covers her mouth. "That's enough! What's the plan?"

"Same tactic Apophis used to hide his earlier crime. Give me the time-dilation ring. As soon as I leave, deliver our earlier selves to this time-place: Pagoda, Mani, tomorrow."

I slip the ring onto my finger and dial the silver circle. What I do now will be concealed in the briefest moment, invisible to all but the most experienced and meticulous eye.

Into the Time Stream, through a portal, arrive at the Office of Technology. The day after the academic conference. Straight to the master console. The energy scan is successful and an access code is generated. I move to the Cosmic Shield control panel and input the code. Request the work logs and search for the day that Priya was with me in this office. Ah. Now where's that override authority? I locate it quickly and erase it. Apophis, your access is denied. Problem solved.

Now for phase two. I pull the energy scans for the same day. There's the video of illusory Priya. Ouch. It's hard to view. Observe her leaving. There's me, stepping forward for the scan. Slow the data to a ridiculous pace … nothing … again, even slower … flicker … a second energy signature … it's him! Instruct the Shield to register this energy signature as Arcturian Enemy. Success!

One last safeguard. I insert the genetic code of the Greys and register it as Arcturian Enemy. All information is automatically uploaded to the military and defence systems. Our planets are now completely protected. My work done, I leave the office and leap back into the Time Stream.

Maya is waiting for me. We enter Atra Atha. "I delivered our earlier selves as instructed. How did everything go?"

I gaze warmly into her eyes. "Mission accomplished."

Sigh of relief. "Shall we check the time line?"

A moment of trepidation. "Yes."

We step into the Immersion and track the planetary lines. Forward … forward … wait for it … there … right on schedule … Apophis reappears with an armed force. The Cosmic Shield is immovable. The Galactic Military reacts with ferocity. The enemy fleet is devastated.

I grab Maya and give her a big hug. "We did it. We did it. We saved our world."

Dancing around in jubilation. Years of accumulated stress beginning to leave my body. Wonderful feelings of freedom and elation.

I suddenly feel so tired. A huge burden has been removed. I slump to the ground and survey the secret room. We really ought to get some reclining leather armchairs in here.

* * *

Maya and I finally get to go home. She is from a time period shortly before mine but her future self will have all the memories. We embrace briefly and make our respective jumps.

Arriving back on Mani fills me with overwhelming emotion. The last time I saw this place it was on the verge of being obliterated. Fear stalked the citizens of this planet. Chaos and destruction rained down on them. It was terrible.

Priya! My brief marriage. It's the one thing that cannot be reinstated. The years away from Mani have helped me come to terms with the loss. But it still hurts.

And then there's Maya. Resolute, independent, quick-tempered daughter of Cronus. Where does she stand regarding me? Is she a close friend? Can there be more? She seems to vacillate between brief moments of intimacy and long periods of indifference. Is it a natural professional distance or self-protectiveness?

My job as Technology Leader no longer has the same appeal. Apprehension and caution have been replaced by an adventurous spirit. There's an expansiveness in me. I need to take care of people. Everything has changed and I am unsure how to proceed.

What will become of my life? I am not the same person who left a beleaguered world all that time ago. My essence has both softened and hardened. I have deep experience and understanding of the Mystery. I have also become worldly-wise, strategic and pragmatic.

I amble along a tree-lined avenue in the glorious sunshine. A wooden bench near the Grand Fountain beckons me. The soft breeze caresses my relaxed body. Hazy rainbows dance across the streams of water. It is truly beautiful.

*Do you mind if I join you?*

"Galactic Leader Savitri. Of course."

*You have been a busy Arcturian.*

I smile broadly. "Is that a good thing?"

Serious countenance. *You have placed us in an awkward position.*

"What do you mean?"

*By resetting the time line. No one on the planet knows about the alternative reality. About the destruction of Arcturus.*

"Oh. I forgot about that."

*It is a silent victory. Shared with only three other people.*

"How did you find out?"

*I have a close relationship with the Time Lord.*

"Aha."

*Let me be clear. We are very proud of you. Arcturus owes you much gratitude.*

"That's good news."

*However, the Planetary and Galactic Leaders have no recollection of the catastrophic event. All they know is what the Time Record reflects: A serious breach of the time law. You and Maya appear to have interfered in numerous time-places, almost indiscriminately.*

"Oh." Brief pause. "How is Maya?"

*I am afraid she is getting the same lecture from her father. Even more difficult, considering the consequences.*

Uncomfortable tingle. "What consequences?"

*We cannot prove that you saved Arcturus. The destruction never happened. The Cosmic Shield never failed. We cannot even locate the pivotal point.*

"I was operating in a time dilation to avoid detection by Apophis."

*There is no evidence in the time lines. And when we interrogated you last week, you never mentioned any time dilation.*

"We had to briefly cloud the minds of our younger versions."

*Younger versions?*

"You do realise that I only returned this morning?"

*I do. Your words are corroborated by Maya's story and the memories of the Time Lord.*

"Cronus. His name is Cronus."

*I am sorry, Indra. Time travel is illegal. Interference is forbidden. The Planetary and Galactic Leaders have no choice but to exile you and Maya.*

Wow. I sigh deeply. There was always that risk. What else could I have done? Avoided responsibility? Stood by and watched my world burn?

"I have no regrets."

*It's time for you to meet someone. Come with me.*

We stroll to the crystal Temple of Arcturus, home of the Galactic Government. Up the steps, through the Gateway, along the enormous high-ceilinged halls. Into the elevator and down a few levels. The ante-chamber scans our energy signatures and demands a password. Guest authorisation is granted. I notice the embossed inscription above the archway: Zakti dAyitva Azaya.

*Power. Responsibility. Virtue.*

"I know. We've been here before."

*Are you aware of the meaning of my name?*

"Savitri? No."

*It means 'relating to the sun'.*

I shrug nonchalantly.

*My body is an unusual blend of genetics. Thanks to this being.*

There stands Cronus and Maya … and the luminous sun-god.

"Ra! What are you doing here?"

He bows respectfully. *Indra, it is good to see you again.*

"Maya, are you alright?"

She nods quietly.

Savitri speaks. *Ra emigrated from Earth's sun to the Arcturian sun millennia ago. The gods of light reside there now. I wonder what could have inspired that journey.*

I raise my hand. That would be me.

*There is a way out. An elegant solution that benefits all parties.*

"Tell me."

*Ra informed us that the gods of light planned to leave Earth soon after 50 BC. Thanks to you, much interference has occurred and will occur on the planet. We need someone to watch over it.*

"You mean a caretaker?"

*We prefer the term Watcher. You and Maya are the perfect candidates.*

"What is the directive?"

*Your mission is to watch over humankind, intervening only when absolutely necessary. You will live on Earth, working quietly and in secret, keeping a close eye on the natural world, genetic codes, advancing technology and politico-socio-economic systems. You will also need to monitor the planet for any sign of the return of Apophis.*

"He was not destroyed by the Galactic Military?"

*Apophis was captured. We confiscated both galaxy's Time Keys. Perhaps it was a desperate escape but he hurled himself into our Time Stream.*

"Without a key? Is that possible?"

Cronus interjects. *Possible only if the person is standing in the Time Chamber. However, it is a one-way ticket, rendering the traveller naked and vulnerable. Whichever time-place he holds in his mind, there he will land. If he manages to keep his mind blank he can hover in the Stream indefinitely.*

"Let me guess. That happened recently. He is still hovering. You have no idea where he will land."

Savitri shifts uncomfortably. *That is the case.*

"You think he will return to Earth?"

*Arcturus is impenetrable. And he does seem to have a preoccupation with Earth.*

I stare at the ceiling. "So what's the deal?"

*You and Maya travel to Earth with Cronus. Arrive 50 BC. You will surrender your Time Keys and all sacred objects. Cronus will carry a message with the seal of the Solar Dynasty. The Ra on Earth will craft two human bodies with a predominance of light-god genetics. Cronus will transfer your consciousness to your new bodies then return with your Arcturian bodies to Mani.*

*Your new bodies will appear human but have the lifespan of a god. Death from natural causes need never concern you. Your bodies will have a crystal skull, allowing communication with the gods of light and access to the multi-dimensions. Cronus will also be able to communicate with you.*

I look across at Maya. "What do you think?"

She nods agreeably. "Our choices are limited. I do have a strong fondness for Earth and feel closely connected to its natural world. And our new bodies will be exquisite."

I sense the sadness in her. There is much she is not saying. But she is right. Our choices are rather limited.

The Galactic Leader is watching me apprehensively. He obviously needs a political resolution. What can he do? Few beings know the truth of our situation.

"When do we leave?"

*As soon as you've said your goodbyes.*

"Two hours will be sufficient."

He glances at Cronus. *How long does Maya need to settle her affairs?*

*That time frame suits us.*

"I have one condition. My first name Indra belongs to my life on Arcturus. Henceforth I will be known by my second name."

*Śakra?*

"Indeed."

* * *

Here we are, back on planet Earth. Many sweet and painful memories are surfacing. Hopefully an exhilarating future stretches before us. Who knows how long we will reside on this world?

Ra has created the promised bodies and we are quickly adapting to the different sensory and operational modalities. The crystal skulls are a wonderful gift and have ignited an idea that has been stirring within me. I suggest to Ra that we establish a Council of Light: Twelve members to assist with the spiritual development and caretaking of Earth. This will also help us track the arrival of any dark energy. He says he will give it some thought.

Maya has reverted to her solitary ways and disappears for months at a time into her beloved nature. Ra has bestowed on her the title *Guardian of the Earth*.

As for me, I decide to return to northeast India. There is something my heart seeks. Perhaps it is a connection to my son. A long trek across the Himalayas finds me in northern Asia. I recall a time line showing that this place will eventually be named Tibet. I assume the role of a monk, gradually coming to favour a saffron-colour robe and a secluded monastery. The lifestyle is peaceful and provides the necessary space to contemplate my life. Ra confers on me the title *Star Child,* a reminder of my celestial origins.

I am gazing across the snow-kissed valley from my lofty perch. The sun is beaming upon the wintry landscape, creating dazzling reflections and ethereal rainbows. Tiny buntings, with their black-and-white heads and chestnut-colour backs, flutter around me. Their soft tweets and gentle songs are blissful company. I take a deep breath and smile. There's a magical feeling in the air. The sense of a great adventure ahead of us.

# Stephen Shaw's Books

**Visit the website**: www.i-am-stephen-shaw.com

**I Am** contains spiritual and mystical teachings from enlightened masters that point the way to love, peace, bliss, freedom and spiritual awakening.

**Heart Song** takes you on a mystical adventure into creating your reality and manifesting your dreams, and reveals the secrets to attaining a fulfilled and joyful life.

**They Walk Among Us** is a love story spanning two realities. Explore the mystery of the angels. Discover the secrets of Love Whispering.

**The Other Side** explores the most fundamental question in each reality. What happens when the physical body dies? Where do you go? Expand your awareness. Journey deep into the Mystery.

**Reflections** offers mystical words for guidance, meditation and contemplation. Open the book anywhere and unwrap your daily inspiration.

**5D** is the Fifth Dimension. Discover ethereal doorways hidden in the fabric of space-time. Seek the advanced mystical teachings.

**Star Child** offers an exciting glimpse into the future on earth. The return of the gods and the advanced mystical teachings. And the ultimate battle of light versus darkness.

**The Tribe** expounds the joyful creation of new Earth. What happened after the legendary battle of Machu Picchu? What is Christ consciousness? What is Ecstatic Tantra?

**The Fractal Key** reveals the secrets of the shamans. This handbook for psychonauts discloses the techniques and practices used in psychedelic healing and transcendent journeys.

Lightning Source UK Ltd.
Milton Keynes UK
UKOW06f0656310817
308313UK00009B/606/P

9 780956 823793